Pulp Fiction

Dana Polan

bfi Publishing

For Marita

First published in 2000 by the
British Film Institute
21 Stephen Street, London W1P 2LN

The British Film Institute promotes greater
understanding of, and access to, film and
moving image culture in the UK.

Series design by Andrew Barron &
Collis Clements Associates

Typeset in Italian Garamond and Swiss 721BT
by D R Bungay Associates, Burghfield, Berks

Printed in Great Britain by
Norwich Colour Print, Drayton, Norfolk

British Library Cataloguing-in-Publication Data
A catalogue record for this book is available
from the British Library
ISBN 0-85170-808-0

Contents

Acknowledgments

My thanks go to my research assistant *extraordinaire* Christine Acham; to my colleague Jeff Sconce for background information; to my patient and judicious editor Rob White. To Marita Sturken, who helps me see the fun and beauty of life, I offer gratitude, admiration, love.

Pulp Fiction

Pulp Fiction is not so much a film as a phenomenon. Winning major prizes, giving rise to an immense culture of obsessive fandom, generating countless wannabes, promoted by its director as an intensely authored work, *Pulp Fiction* burns and bursts its way into its historical moment as an inescapable signpost of its age. The significance of *Pulp Fiction* is not located objectively in the structure of the work itself but in the resonances this work has – both for its admirers and its detractors. For these viewers, the significance and value of *Pulp Fiction* are generally to be found not in any message the film imparts nor in any political position it explicitly adheres to but in its reaching beyond meaning and moralism to offer up a sheer cinematic spectacle, a fun-house experience of vibrant sights and sounds. Those who like this film do so because it doesn't seem to have anything to say and renders cinematic experience as pure play. Those who dislike it dislike it for the very same reasons, seeing the deliberate cool superficiality of *Pulp Fiction* as a symptom of the empty post-modernity of our age. Or they see the film as hiding some real political issues – for example, around masculinity and race – behind a seductive veneer of spectacle that it claims is beyond politics.

'And they called it puppy love' (Paul Anka)

The NFT [National Film Theatre] is usually the haunt of bookish, serious-minded *cineastes*, but this occasion was different. 'We had 3,000 applications for tickets from members alone,' said Brian Robinson, a spokesman for the NFT. 'From early December onward, the phones didn't stop ringing. Every other call was people asking for Tarantino tickets. The main NFT theatre, capacity 450, was packed, but another 162 people in a smaller adjacent theatre saw the interview and question-and-answer session on video screens. … Tarantino fans started lining up outside the NFT 10 hours before the interview session.[1]

There are many markers of the *Pulp Fiction* phenomenon. Numerous Internet websites, for example, are dedicated to Tarantino and *Pulp*

Fiction – dozens if not hundreds. Thus, a random check using 'Quentin + Tarantino' as my keywords produced a list of over ten thousand citings of the name. There's an intense proliferation of sites overwhelmingly dedicated to the man and this film.

And we can understand this notion of 'dedicated' in at least three revealing ways. First, there is the somewhat neutral sense in which the sites pick Tarantino and/or *Pulp Fiction* as their object of attention, no matter the approach they take or the attitude they adopt or the value judgments they make. In the same way that we can speak of a 'dedicated' phone to refer to a telephone or a line that is given over to one function, to one act of communication, irrespective of what that might be, the first significant thing about all the web attention to Tarantino and *Pulp Fiction* is simply that it is there, that there is so much of it, that so many people have chosen to dedicate so much time to building these websites no matter what they end up saying on them.

To be sure, we can expect in our cyber-age that every subject will have multiple websites devoted to it, but the number of Tarantino and Tarantino-film sites is recognisably excessive. We might pinpoint this by contrasting it with the relative paucity of sites on other worthy subjects. For instance, the wildly popular HBO Mafia series *The Sopranos* seems to me easily to be one of the best things television has ever done, and a number of its qualities bear similarity to the filmic world of Tarantino: the veering back and forth between humour and violence in ways that keep audiences guessing ('Should I be laughing? Should I be cringing?'); the portrayal and dissection of myths of masculinity; a post-modern concern with citation and the sense that in a media age one acts according to established entertainment models (the gangsters in *The Sopranos* are endlessly comparing themselves to *The Godfather* or to Pacino in *Scarface*); an obsessive construction of a self-contained world peopled by a few select characters whose interaction generates new story possibilities; a sheer bravado of style and acting and narrative confidence that can make both works stand out from typical cinematic and televisual fare.

But *The Sopranos* has generated little cyber-adulation; there are few fan sites, and almost none treat the show with the rigour and detail that

Tarantino's works garner. One senses that a primary factor in this fandom is generational. As I'll suggest, a personality like Quentin Tarantino (who interestingly is himself quite cyber-illiterate) and a film like *Pulp Fiction* seem perfect for a historical moment populated by cyber-geeks for whom the web comes as a veritable godsend to give them 'a life'. Indeed, we might note in passing that in going through the list of websites dedicated to Tarantino and his films, one discovers that quite a number of them are no longer active. One senses that for their website authors the Tarantino world fulfilled specific obsessive needs at a biographical moment but then life went on, new concerns (or perhaps obsessions) arose and the Tarantino obsession was put aside. Tarantino is clearly a director of important transitional life-moments for many fans.

Whatever the judgment passed on Tarantino and his films on this or that website, the sheer proliferation of sites suggests that many people find here something to talk about, something to dedicate time to, to expend energy and effort on. For the most part, indeed, a very great deal of the Tarantino web-talk is intensely laudatory. Here, a second sense of 'dedication' emerges. In the way that an author might dedicate a book to someone – might imagine it, that is, in honour of someone (for example, a benefactor) – many of the Quentin Tarantino websites seem to be presented as virtual salutations to the director, acts of love offered up on the altar of auteurist admiration. There is in all this web activity a feverish sort of fandom, but one that also blurs into obsessive identification as if many of the web designers don't simply want to announce their love of Tarantino but want to be like him – indeed, to be him. In passing, we might note that obsessive fandom has its corollary in Tarantino films themselves, where many characters find it necessary to discuss endlessly and in great detail the things they love in their culture (food, celebrities, cult films, and so on).

For a typical example of these labours of love, take a look at the aptly named website 'www.godamongdirectors.com/tarantino' (by Kale Morton), which sports a front-page quotation from Tarantino himself: 'The coolest web [site]'. The site includes (and this is only a very partial list): a big section of FAQs (Frequently Asked Questions) about

Tarantino films; a schedule of upcoming television presentations of his films; transcripts of interviews; something called the 'Tarantinoverse' ('a comparison of QT's films and compares and contrasts aspects which seem to carry into all of Tarantino's Films'[*sic*]); reprints of major articles; scripts for all the films; downloadable sounds from the movies (for example, the Big Mac speech from *Pulp Fiction*); downloadable clips and trailers and various forms of arcania (for example, a 'discussion, with examples of trunkshots in Tarantino films'); or a 'comprehensive' analysis of an unclear plot development in one of the films – namely, what happened to *Reservoir Dogs*' Mr Pink 'once he left the building with the diamonds'). To be precise, we discover that Tarantino is only one of several 'godsamongdirectors' – each of whom gets his own section – but the full list – Robert Rodriguez, Martin Scorsese, John Woo, Kevin Smith – is revealing: these are hip directors of a violent cool but also of a baroque visual messiness, who can tap into the fantasies of a generation and become veritable obsessions.

And here we encounter a third sense of 'dedication': by this, I refer to the sheer amount of time that these labours of love seem to have involved. Unlike a book dedication where one quick phrase can announce an author's gratitude or devotion, the Tarantino websites are literally labours in which vast amounts of energy evidently have been dedicated to create rich cyber-universes filled with complicated graphics and audio samplings, bountiful text given over to detailed analysis, bits of humour, quotations and bibliography, electronic links, and so on.

(Interestingly, just as Tarantino films frequently cite from other works, the websites recycle much of their information. For example, the same FAQ list is repeated verbatim on a number of sites.)

Just as the Tarantino films – *Pulp Fiction* especially – build up self-contained universes in which a few select people interact and generate new narrative possibilities, so too the websites seem caught up in a virtually science-fictional universe-building as they blend image and words in rich patterns of interactivity and in which a limited number of elements combine in ever new permutations to create bountiful worlds of possibility (each click of the mouse will bring the web-surfer ever more Tarantino information as sites embed text within text, bounties of information within their pages).

The effort of these web designers can seem very dedicated indeed. Take, for instance, what must be one of the most striking cases of fan dedication, the *Fox Force Five* website ('http://nextdch.mty.itesm.mx/~plopezg/FFF3/FFF.html'). Designed by Patricio Lopez-Guzman, a twenty-something communication major in Mexico, this site is, depending on your point of view, either a fascinating venture in web creativity (it proudly sports an award for 'Top 5% of all websites' from the 'GIST. web pick') or a curious eccentricity that signals the obsessiveness of so many lives lived out in cyberspace.

Fox Force Five, you may remember, is the TV show that *Pulp Fiction*'s Mia Wallace (Uma Thurman) tells Vince Vega (John Travolta) she did a pilot for, only to have the option on the show dropped by the network. In Mia's words, 'It was a show about a team of female secret agents called '*Fox Force Five*'. ... Fox, as we're a bunch of foxy chicks. Force, as in we're a force to be reckoned with. Five, as in there's one ... two ... three ... four ... five of us.' In the film, *Fox Force Five* is discussed only in passing but it appears to serve several narrative functions. The pilot is first mentioned (but not by name) by Jules Winnfield (Samuel L. Jackson), who is describing Mia to Vince and giving some of her background. Here, the reference helps explain something about Mia (she's a failed Hollywood wannabe). It also enables us to learn something about Vince: namely, that his relation to popular

culture is a bit erratic. Vince, as he himself admits, doesn't watch much
television – potentially a sin in the Tarantino universe where so much of
what one is comes from the popular culture one has ingested. Tarantino
himself in a 1993 interview made a declaration about popular culture
that would itself become dialogue in *Pulp Fiction*:

I don't think it's the worst thing in the world. That's what makes America
what it is, what gives it its charm, part of its personality. It's a junk-food
culture. … I'd never been to other countries before this year, but I've now
been to other countries, and I love going into McDonalds. The difference? In
the Paris McDonalds, they serve beer. And they don't call it a Quarter
Pounder, because they have the metric system there: Le Royale with
Cheese! They don't know what a fucking quarter pounder is![2]

When Mia and Vince discuss *Fox Force Five* as they wait for their meal at
the diner Jack Rabbit Slim's, the mention again has several functions. It
is one of the random subjects of conversation that Mia and Vince use to
break the ice and get their evening going. Such shared reference to mass
culture is one of the primary sources of sociability in the Tarantino
universe. And once again, such allusion reiterates how this universe is
one in which works of mass culture (especially the schlocky cultural
forms of the 70s that make *Fox Force Five* sound so familiar) are
inescapable points of reference for its inhabitants (even if Vince doesn't

'It was a show about a team of female secret agents called *Fox Force Five*'

watch current television, he is certainly up on his popular culture and, as we learn in Jack Rabbit Slim's, can easily distinguish a Marilyn Monroe from a Jayne Mansfield from a Mamie Van Doren). Finally, a joke from *Fox Force Five* that Mia refuses to tell in Jack Rabbit Slim's becomes later a mark of their bond when finally she recounts it to Vincent at the end of their momentous evening.

But even though we see how the references to *Fox Force Five* serve several functions, the overall effect is one of inconsequential allusion, one more moment in which Tarantino characters are shown to live out their lives through mass cultural reference (to take another example, when Jules has to talk down Honey [Amanda Plummer] as they face off against each other with big guns, he tells her to be 'cool', specifically, as he puts it, like Fonzie in the TV show *Happy Days*).

This inconsequentiality is quite different from the fetishistic intensity of the *Fox Force Five* site. The conceit here is that the show actually existed, and the site includes – among other things – a detailed character profile and biography for each member of the *Fox Force Five* team (with the joke given away by the fact that the foxy women's leader is said to be the mysterious Q. T., a man of 'slick charisma, renegade charm and high respect among government female employees'); an interview with one of the show's actresses; reviews of the show; a schedule of showings of the show; a list of FAQs (for example, what do we know about the supposed *Fox Force Five* TV movie, which the website

'Nobody's gonna hurt anybody'

tells us 'was an attempt to revive the *Fox Force Five* series in the 90s'?); a breakdown of the pilot episode; a description of a '*Fox Force Five* game'; a statistical count of recurrent shots (for example, the number of times the force gets 'a new member that is not killed in the same episode'); and, most astoundingly, a several-page list, complete with detailed imagery, of *Fox Force Five* merchandise (T-shirts, lunchboxes, coffee mugs, all festooned with the *FF5* logo).

The jokiness of the *Fox Force Five* website becomes quickly apparent (for example, we're told that the *FF5* lunchbox sells for $777.77 and is 'great for transporing [*sic*] anything from spam, to jelly sandwiches. Made with 10% asvestos [*sic*] to protect your food from the afternoon heat'). It would be easy to dismiss this as one more weird bit of ephemera that the indulgences of the web encourage and enable. But this site – and others like it – capture something very particular about Quentin Tarantino and a film like *Pulp Fiction*: he is a director who makes films that arouse intense passion and an emotional investment that easily tips into obsession.

To be sure, not all of this passion is favourable toward the director. As strong as the love for Tarantino and his films is the vehement hatred for his world that many feel. Note, for example, how the awarding of the Palme d'Or, the top prize at the 1994 Cannes Film Festival, to *Pulp Fiction* was received by a woman in the audience, who kept screaming almost to the point of hysteria that this was a 'scandale' and that Tarantino was a 'fasciste'. Or take, for instance, film scholar and critic Robin Wood's virulently aggressive digression on *Pulp Fiction* within a long analysis of Greg Araki's *The Doom Generation* (a film which Wood applauds):

Tarantino has shown himself obviously incapable of making a film as intelligent and beautiful [as *The Doom Generation*] ... *Pulp Fiction* is an entirely spurious work, the product of a mind/sensibility that will probably now (thanks to the premature adulation) never transcend its adolescent immaturity, seeking at all points to involve the audience in its complacent sense of its own cleverness, its own emptiness and cynicism.[3]

The Doom Generation

The denunciations can move from mere aesthetic disapproval to moral outrage. For example, for columnist Fintan O'Toole writing in the *Guardian*, 'Tarantino is of considerable pathological interest. His films should be studied as Exhibit A in the museum of post-modern moral vacuity.'[4]

On the web, controversy has sprouted up over the 'Anti-Tarantino' site of Mike White (http://www.impossiblefunky.com/qt/), who argues that what fans see as hip quotation in Tarantino films is actually direct plagiarism. Chronicling the production and often virulent reception of the short films White made that compared scenes in *Reservoir Dogs* to ones in the Hong Kong film *City on Fire* and numerous moments in *Pulp Fiction* to a whole series of films (for example, Sonny Chiba action films, in which the hero quotes the Bible before dispatching his enemies), the Anti-Tarantino site sets out energetically to temper the praise for Tarantino as an original voice in cinema. What is striking, then, is the sheer violence with which fans have responded to what they evidently perceive as a personal attack – not only on their idol but on themselves, since they have so clearly projected themselves into him and into his world: the guest book for the Anti-Tarantino site is filled with comments such as the following:

Tarantino could be in the future a Orson Welles or a Hitchcock. Leave tarantino alone, get a life … You fucking animal, you must be the most jealous gimp on earth. Try to learn a bit asshole … and stop watching Van Damme movies, neard. FUCKING GIMP.

You really suck you fukin prick Tarantino kicks ass.

WHERE DO U GET THE GALL TO CALL ONE OF THE GREATEST DIRECTORS A PLAGERIST??? HUH, YOU SHOULD HAVE YOUR ASS BEATEN SEVERLY!!!! … ALL YOU DO I BET IS FIND THE FLAWS IN PEOPLES WORK, THAT IS JUST SICKENING … I SINCERELY HOPE YOU FIND A LIFE. [sic]

These are only a few of the endless paeans to Tarantino that show up on Anti-Tarantino (and, to be fair, there are several defences of Mike White, although they are fewer in number and far weaker in passion and energy). One intriguing recurrent feature is the charge that the anti-Tarantinist doesn't have a life (as one of the other postings puts it, 'Leave Quentin alone! He's a great director! You guys should unplug a while and get some fresh air!'). Such comments seem highly ironic, in that it is easy to imagine that many of the Tarantino fans are themselves people who passionately trade rich, multivaried life experiences for overbearing obsessive immersion in the cool Tarantino universe and its reinvention on the web.

'Signs, signs, everywhere a sign' (Five-Man Electrical Band)

It's necessary to go further and try to give some content to this passion, to explain just how it manifests itself. First of all, as the fixation on minutiae in the *Fox Force Five* website suggests, Tarantino fandom is directly fetishistic. That is, it latches on to little moments of the films and examines them intensely, rigorously. This fetishistic enactment of 'trivial pursuits', in which details become sites of extreme investment, shows up too in many of the websites on Tarantino and *Pulp Fiction*. For example, one recurrent question from the FAQs has to do with the seeming illogic of a professional killer like Vincent leaving his machine gun out in the kitchen and going to the bathroom while he is alone, thus making himself vulnerable and giving Butch (Bruce Willis) the opportunity to kill him. The answer – one designed to warm the heart of any textual analyst

– is that Vincent wasn't really expecting to be alone: if you look closely (and stopping the videotape at this point will help!) at the following scene when Butch encounters Vincent's boss Marsellus (Ving Rhames), you will notice that Marsellus is carrying two cups of coffee, one of which he was probably bringing back to Vincent (here, it helps to have figured out the chronology of the film and realised that Jules has by now quit the life of crime and left Vincent partnerless, thus requiring Marsellus to step in). The machine gun is Marsellus's and Vincent went to the bathroom thinking his boss would be around to protect him.

This poring over little bits of the film can certainly seem to come from the obsessions that fans bring to the film, but it is also necessary to realise that the structure and style of *Pulp Fiction* (and *Reservoir Dogs*) enable such fetishism and derive much of their significance in parading details before the spectator. Breathlessly, many moments in *Pulp Fiction* seem to flow over the spectator, who tries to take from them what he or she can. The first level of such detail has to do with a proliferation of references and allusions – especially to the world of popular culture. Vincent's energised walk through Jack Rabbit Slim's – done in a long take in which the camera swirls through the scene while impersonators of famous movie stars slide past him as he tries, sometimes with success, sometimes with bewilderment, to recognise them all – could almost serve as a metaphor for the activity of the spectator, at whom the film throws dozens and dozens of references. For the spectator, there's little major intellectual work to be done here (unlike a second function of details in

Marsellus with coffee

Pulp Fiction, as we'll see in a moment): you either get the reference or you don't, and there is a sliding scale of difficulty in the obscurity of the allusion and its source. Getting the reference allows entry into a private club, this being one of the functions of cult culture (it's like a priesthood with procedures of inclusion and exclusion for membership). Jack Mathews puts it this way in a commentary in the *Los Angeles Times*: 'For viewers who went in expecting a conventional movie, it must have been like walking into a club where everyone knew the password and secret handshake but them.'[5] A negative review of the film in the *Denver Post* renders explicit the feeling one can have at not gaining entrance into this cult universe:

There is no reason for the existence of this movie other than as a primer in pop culture cool. This divides the audience into those who get it and those who don't, rather than those who like it and those who don't. When Samuel L. Jackson calls a frightened young man with long bangs 'Flock of Seagulls', we either laugh at the reference to the lead singer of that band or the remark whizzes by. Tarantino fills his movies with so much cultural arcanum that only a junkie like himself could possibly get all the references. But the more you get, the cooler you are. Tarantino's films are like hazing rituals for admission into the cult of attitude.[6]

In passing, drawn from the web and writings on Tarantino, here are some of the popular culture references in *Pulp Fiction*: Marsellus stepping out

'Jack Rabbit Slim's, the big mama of 50s diners'

into the crosswalk and recognising the fugitive Butch is like the boss spotting Marion Bates trying to leave town in *Psycho*; Marsellus rising up from the ground after Butch has tried to run him over is filmed like the endless return of the psycho-killer/serial-monster in films like *Halloween*; the rape-by-rednecks scene harkens back to *Deliverance* (one of the earliest films Quentin Tarantino saw); Vincent's dancing in Jack Rabbit Slim's is a reference back to all the films in which Travolta is given a moment to show off his dancing talents, from *Saturday Night Fever* and *Grease* all the way up to *Look Who's Talking*, where the dance is already a post-modern reference to the actor as much as to the character, and some people have even seen reminiscences of Olivia Newton-John's dance steps from *Grease* in Mia's moves with Vincent (Tarantino also based some of Mia's moves on the dance of one of the cats in the

Reinventing Travolta

animated film, *The Aristocats*); the story the Christopher Walken
character tells of his incarceration in Vietnam refers to *The Deerhunter*
and what happens to the Walken character there; when Jules and Vincent
have to clean up the remains of Marvin, they go to the house of Jules's
friend Jimmie (Quentin Tarantino himself), which some see as a
reference to *Jules and Jim*[mie], a masterwork of the French New Wave
cinema that is so central to Tarantino (there's a post-modern genealogy
here in which the classic American films noirs are reworked by New
Wavers like Godard and Truffaut which are then themselves reworked in
a film like *Pulp Fiction*; the endless philosophising by characters as they
engage in or contemplate acts of violence could have come out of any
Godard film); the glow of the briefcase that Vincent and Jules retrieve
from the kids radiates like the one in *Kiss Me Deadly* and like the car
trunk in *Repo Man* (Tarantino films are filled with emphatic scenes of
trunks being opened and closed); Winston Wolf (Harvey Keitel) seems to

Allusions (1):
Kiss Me Deadly

be the same character, a cleaner-upper of death scenes, that he played in *Point of No Return* (which, to continue the recycling, was itself a remake of a French film, *La Femme Nikita*); impeccably dressed in his tuxedo in the early hours of the morning and zooming around in a fast car as he arrives in perfect composure to solve problems, Wolf is perhaps also a reference to the elegant professionalism of James Bond.

Some of the references are even more arcane: Mia's hairstyle is like that of Anna Karina in several Godard films – such as *Bande à part*, in which the characters do a vibrant dance like that in Jack Rabbit Slim's (Tarantino's production company is named A Band Apart). Some of the allusions are less to specific films than to genres. For instance, the story of Butch, the fighter who decides not to go down for the count, has numerous antecedents in Hollywood (most famously, the films noirs *Body*

Allusions (2): Anna Karina in Godard's *Vivre sa vie*

Allusions (3): John
Carpenter's *Halloween*

and Soul and *The Set Up*), while Tarantino himself has said in interviews
that the following of Jules and Vincent through their day after the hit as
they have to mop up Marvin's body is intended as a sort of
deconstruction (although this is not his word) of endless films in which
killers knock someone off, after which we cut abruptly to another locale
where they go on their merry way without a care in the world.

Beyond these fairly direct allusions, we might note that the script
for *Pulp Fiction* frequently sets up an action or a scene in terms of some
popular culture work or film genre it wants to gain the feel of: thus, for
instance, we're told on the first page that Honey Bunny and Pumpkin's
dialogue is to be said in a 'rapid pace *His Girl Friday* style', while Jules
and Vincent go to their first hit with 'their long matching overcoats
practically dragging on the ground', an image out of Sergio Leone that in
fact was not kept for the actual filming. Similarly, when Lance has to
explain to Vincent how to stab Mia with a needle to save her from a

heroin overdose, he 'demonstrates a stabbing motion, which looks like the "The Shape" killing its victims in *Halloween*', and some people have also seen a reference to vampire movies with their stake-in-the-heart (interestingly, this sets up an allusion within an allusion: the stabbing brings Mia back to life, rather than turning her into a victim, but she springs up with the zombie-like pallor of her skin and the hollow of her eyes rendering her like one of those creatures that refuse to die in so many zombie-monster films of the 80s). In filming, Tarantino frequently takes some other popular work as inspiration for the feel or look of an element in his film, even if the reference is not a direct one. For example, he has declared that the character of Butch is modelled on the Ralph Meeker character in *Kiss Me Deadly* and even more on the Aldo Ray figure in Jacques Tourneur's 1956 noir classic *Nightfall*.

Allusions (4): *Nightfall*

We might also note that arguments could be made for the derivative and referential nature of the film's overall structure (a structure of achronology, interrupted narratives, shifts in tone) and not just of this or that character or line of dialogue. Thus, Tarantino (in an interview with French writer Jean-Pierre Deloux) likens *Pulp Fiction*'s fragmentary and interrupted nature to the specific structure of the literature of pulp fiction and the casual forms of consumption it encourages:

[a pulp fiction novel] is a novel you could buy for a dime, that you read in the bus while going to work. At work, you would put it in your back pocket, you'd sit on it all day long, and you'd continue reading it on the bus on the way home, and when you finished it you gave it to a friend or you'd throw it in the garbage.[7]

Likewise, Pat Dowell in *Cineaste* offers an intriguing argument that the structure of *Pulp Fiction* derives from TV sitcoms (revealingly, beyond the reference to Fonzie in *Happy Days*, the script included a scene where Mia makes Vincent choose between *The Brady Bunch* and *The Partridge Family* and between *Bewitched* and *I Dream of Jeannie*). In Dowell's words:

The structure of *Pulp Fiction* is not so new as it looks. It should be familiar to any television watcher, for it is our psychological accommodations to TV's dramatic shape that Tarantino exploits for his narrative surprises. Every day Americans are quite at home with stories that come to a rest, divided into

'… a novel you could buy for a dime'

segments to be interrupted by other stories, and then resume. The interruptions are called commercials and increasingly they are commercials for other stories, both on television and in the movies. Channel surfing also segments the stories we watch. In *Pulp Fiction* Tarantino starts episodes and lets them come to what feel like commercial breaks. The setup scene of Honey Bunny and Pumpkin in the coffee shop planning their robbery is exactly like the tease that opens most television shows before the first commercial; audiences don't expect it in a movie and so don't frame it as such, but, after surfing in and out of other episodes, Tarantino eventually returns to it.[8]

Certainly, it could be argued that a number of the plots in *Pulp Fiction* are like versions of TV sitcom that have mutated into film noir. For example, the whole of the segment entitled 'The Bonnie Situation' – in which the hitmen are reduced to virtual adolescence (even in their manner of dress) as they try to clean up a mess (in this case, a body and a bloodied car) before Bonnie comes home – has the structure of those sorts of sitcoms in which kids get into some mess while the parents are away and then spend the whole segment or episode trying to make things right before time runs out and the figures of authority return. This, too, is the structure of the sequence in which Vincent has to save Mia from overdosing and make sure the authority figure Marsellus doesn't find out. Interestingly, Vincent can only save Mia by taking her to Lance's suburban home – here, a veritable bastion of mass culture with the TV always on, the inhabitants decked out in popular-culture T-shirts, the detritus of consumer society spread out all over (including, for those who obsessively look for details – get ready to hit freeze on the remote control! – board games of Life and Operation in the living room where Vincent engages in the medical procedure to save Mia). When he crashes into the house with his car and carries Mia in, it is as if Vincent is bringing the harsher, violent world of *Pulp Fiction* into the seemingly safer haven of the domestic sitcom. As critic Sarah Kerr puts it in her review of the film:

The drug-dealer and his wife are a low-life amoral echo of Ralph and Alice Kramden [from the working-class sitcom, *The Honeymooners*] and all the bickering TV couples who followed them. The fact that the subject of tonight's argument is a near-dead woman's blood-and-drool covered body and that resolving tonight's dilemma requires stabbing her heart with a syringe only ups the ante.[9]

But if the spotting of the allusions is an effortless activity that you either get or don't, which therefore doesn't really involve work on the part of the spectator, another level of fetishistic obsession – and another level of the film's appeal – has to do with the more active labour of figuring out *Pulp Fiction*'s various puzzles. Certainly, some of the interactivity of the film works only for the trivialist (for most of us, it would never occur to wonder why Vincent is alone in the bathroom with his machine gun on the counter), who can thereby flaunt his or her (but usually his, given the ideal audience for this nerdy obsessiveness) special knowledge (to take another example drawn from the web, freeze-framing shows that there are already bullet holes in the wall before the young man empties his revolver at Jules and Vincent). The very structure of *Pulp Fiction* is a puzzle, its unveiling of the plot achronologically asking spectators to figure out just what happened, and when, chronologically. One could debate just how avant-gardist this playing with temporality is – interestingly, Tarantino himself in interviews argues that the film is easily accessible even with its achronology, and it is true that the film was able to cross over from independent film cult classic to mainstream hit – but there is no doubt that it encourages an active spectator who is given the job of putting the pieces of a puzzle together.

In passing, here, sorted out, is the chronology of the film: early one morning, Jules and Vincent are sent to retrieve a briefcase for their crime boss Marsellus and do a hit on some young kids (probably college guys) who have failed to return the mysterious briefcase to Marsellus. One of the kids had been in the bathroom and he charges out unloading his gun, but all the bullets miss Jules and Vincent and he is shot dead. Afterwards, as they are driving away, Marvin, the mole who set up the kids, is killed in the back seat when Vincent's gun goes off accidentally. They call Marsellus for help and he dispatches Winston Wolf to meet them at Jimmie's house. After Mr Wolf helps them clean up the mess and drop off the cadaver and car, Vincent and Jules go off to a diner for breakfast. Here, they discuss whether or not the bullets missing them was a miracle. Honey Bunny and Pumpkin try to hold up the diner and have a stand-off with Vincent and Jules, who lets them go. Vincent and Jules go to a club, where Jules gives the briefcase to Marsellus, who has just been telling Butch the boxer to take a dive in his next boxing match. Vincent and Butch have a little run-in.

The next narrative development is not shown but implied: Jules leaves the life of crime and no longer figures in the story (the implication is that in the nightclub he tells Marsellus he is quitting and then does so). In the evening, Vincent goes to dealer Lance's house for a heroin score and then shows up at Marsellus's place to take Mia out. Vincent and Mia go out to Jack Rabbit Slim's. When they return from the restaurant, Mia nearly overdoses on heroin. Vincent rushes her to Lance, who is able to save her. Mia and Vincent say goodbye outside her house.

On the night of the fight (which night isn't clear), Butch disobeys Marsellus, kills his opponent in the ring, and flees in a cab. Marsellus summons Vincent and assigns him to track down Butch. Meanwhile, the cab takes Butch to the motel where he and his girlfriend Fabienne are hiding out. The next morning Butch realises that Fabienne has left his father's watch back at his old apartment. He goes to get it and encounters Vincent, whom he kills. Driving away, he has a run-in with Marsellus and after a chase both end up in a redneck pawnshop. They are abused by the rednecks and Marsellus is raped. Butch manages to untie himself, but instead of fleeing he rescues Marsellus, who promises torture for the surviving redneck. With accounts settled between him and Marsellus, Butch returns to Fabienne and they ride off on one of the rednecks' chopper.

'You were always on my mind, you were always on my mind' (Elvis Presley)

Pulp Fiction's shifts in temporality complement shifts in tone that can challenge complacent viewing. The narrative of the film endlessly veers

Allusions (5): *The Texas Chain Saw Massacre*

off in unexpected directions: for example, we don't expect Mia and Vincent's evening out to end in a drug overdose; we don't expect the Butch–Marsellus battle to take a detour into an encounter with redneck rapists; we don't expect Vincent's gun to go off and turn the last story into a 'waste disposal' issue. This constant shifting of tone and plot makes *Pulp Fiction* into a veritable guessing game where the viewer keeps wondering what will happen next. In film critic Roger Ebert's words:

The method of the movie is to involve its characters in sticky situations, and then let them escape into stickier ones, which is how the boxer and the mob boss end up together as the captives of weird leather freaks in the basement of a gun shop. ... Most of the action in the movie comes under the heading of crisis control.[10]

This shifting quality of the narrative gets a sort of condensed parody in the scene where Butch looks for a weapon to unleash on the rednecks. It is already a surprise that he has decided to stay and save Marsellus, and now we watch as he escalates from one implement of destruction to another, going – as some commentators have claimed – from the genre of horror (a chainsaw à la *Texas Chain Saw Massacre*) to that of the Japanese yakuza film (a samurai sword à la Paul Schrader's script for *The Yakuza*). Tarantino himself claims as one influence for the structure of the movie the world of spaghetti Westerns:

The stories in the movie remind me of *The Good, the Bad and the Ugly*. You're following these two guys, you're following them, then suddenly they turn a corner and BOOM! they're in the middle of a civil war! They're in another movie! How the fuck did they get in there? They don't know and you're just as confused as they are.[11]

Allusions (6): *The Yakuza*

We might note that the film's characters frequently gaze at plot shifts with astonishment and become veritable stand-ins for the spectator, who is trying to figure out each twist and turn of the plot and tone. I've already cited the sequence when Vincent moves through Jack Rabbit Slim's with bemused bewilderment as mass-culture references flow past him. Indeed, for all his hitman professionalism, Vincent is also a character who is continuously getting caught unawares, a figure who often misses out on major narrative developments because he was in the bathroom, caught, as film scholar Sharon Willis says, with 'his pants down' (the phrase is also Pumpkin's at the beginning of *Pulp Fiction* as he contemplates robbing the diner, unaware that Vincent is in the bathroom).[12] Like a spectator who leaves a movie for a moment to get a smoke or go to the rest room, Vincent is endlessly leaving and then finding, upon his return, that all the terms of the situation have changed: in the diner, he discovers that a robbery and stand-off have occurred during his absence; while he goes off to the bathroom at Mia's, she overdoses and puts him in danger with Marsellus; when he uses Butch's bathroom, Butch returns, finds Vincent's machine gun and kills him. Like the spectator, Vincent discovers that the narrative of *Pulp Fiction* is endlessly one step ahead of him.

Similarly, Butch is often a figure who looks at the world in amazement and tries to follow it through its unpredictable mutations. Easily one of the most sympathetic figures in the film, Butch becomes a

Vincent's endless movement

relay for the audience's viewing. Indeed, he is given the greatest number of point-of-view shots in the film, so that we discover many elements of the story along with him. Moreover, these shots are often emphasised by an emphatic camera movement – usually toward the object of vision – as when Butch finds Vincent's machine gun on the kitchen counter, as if to mark the momentousness of subjectivity all the more strongly. Butch is a figure directly caught up in shifts in narrative and in tone. For example, the whole of his adventure in retrieving the watch is a whirlwind of unpredictability that we share with him: the surprise of Vincent being at his apartment, of Marsellus crossing the road in front of him (and then of rising 'from the dead' after Butch tries to run him over), of the pawnshop harbouring evil rednecks, and on and on. Additionally, Butch is the figure most associated with moments where the film abruptly shifts status from dream or fantasy to reality. Twice, we see him wake up in startled panic and confusion from a narrative that takes place in another realm (first, he awakens from the 'flashback' in which he is told by Captain Koons about the legacy of the gold watch to find himself in the locker room before his big fight; then, he falls asleep in the motel room with Fabienne only to be bolted awake by the shots and explosions of the action movie she's watching the next morning on TV). Processing the permutations of reality and its flirtations with realms of surreality, Butch is a figure who tries to understand and master shifts in the narrative world around him.

Butch's surprise at seeing Marsellus

Through its shifts, *Pulp Fiction*, in many ways, is a roller coaster of a movie, blending moments of calm before the storm (for example, long scenes of discussion and dialogue, moments of repose in home or in food establishments) with bursts of vibrant action (scenes of violence – robberies, shoot-outs, chases, fistfights, beatings and rapes, accidental killings – but also other forms of energetic display – for instance, frenetic dances and drug overdoses). These wild and unpredictable shifts in the movie account for much of the emotional investment that spectators make in it, since this is a film in which one cannot confidently predict where things are going. Indeed, the film seems deliberately to play with the audience and keeps it on its toes.

Take, for instance, the episode at the end of the film where we loop back to the opening scene where Honey Bunny and Pumpkin plan to hold up the diner (obsessives will note that the dialogue is slightly different in the supposed repetition of Honey Bunny leaping up with her gun; and virtuoso obsessives will have noted that in the opening scene between Honey Bunny and Pumpkin, we can see Vincent going off to the bathroom in one shot). The end scene in the diner is one moment where plot elements come together to give the spectators some glimpse of a narrative logic and thereby make them think they're in control of things (the first time I saw *Pulp Fiction*, I remember coming close to emitting a triumphant 'Aha' when I realised that the film had looped back on itself). But even this momentary mastery of the plot doesn't add up to much, since we still don't know how the stand-off between the hitmen and would-be robbers will turn out. To be sure, if we have been attentive to the play of chronology, we know that Vincent survives the encounter (since he is killed later by Butch), but we don't have any information on Jules's fate, let alone Honey Bunny or Pumpkin's. When, for instance, Jules begins once again to recite his 'Ezekiel' speech, the film continues to hold out the possibility that Jules will shoot Honey Bunny or Pumpkin as he had all his previous victims. (Interestingly, the script of *Pulp Fiction* actually has Jules kill them both, along with what it terms a 'Surfer patron', who is accidentally shot by Honey Bunny when she falls. Suddenly, though, a flash lets us realise this is Jules's imagining

what he could do but now won't, since he has given up the life of a killer. Certainly, this play with illusion and reality would have been in keeping with the film's general disorientation of the spectator.)

'Day after day, I stay locked up in my room' (The Temptations)

If the initial manifestations of passion for *Pulp Fiction* of the sort we find on the web have to do with fetishising it (catching its allusions, trying to figure out its chronology, getting caught up in the puzzle of its plot twists), a second might be explained by the fact that so much of this passion is being worked out in places precisely like the web. In many ways, *Pulp Fiction* seems a perfect film for an age (historical but also biological) in which so much happens in electronic dimensions, where one of the places to get a life (now that so many malls are closing down) is in cyberspace.

At first, to argue that *Pulp Fiction* is a film for the cyber-generation may seem paradoxical. We can note, for instance, how insignificant a role any image of advanced technology plays in the film. *Pulp Fiction* is not *The Matrix*. Aside from a few cell phones (for example, a reference to an astute bank robber who used one in his heist) and some television sets, *Pulp Fiction* shows us a virtually Luddite world with nary a computer terminal in sight, where most of the work is the very physical, even mucky hands-on effort of killing people or disposing of their bodies.

To be sure, there is a hint of hi-tech in Marsellus and Mia's abode, where Mia first greets Vincent through an intercom system after spying

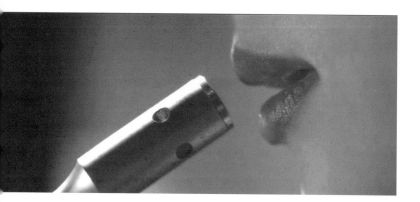

on him with surveillance cameras (a scene cut from the film's release version had Mia meeting Vincent with a camcorder through which she tapes his answers to questions about popular culture). But even Mia is made to participate in a minor anti-technology joke that runs through the film. Most of the music in *Pulp Fiction* is shown to be diegetic (that is, it arises from within the world of the action, rather than being played over it) and the sources are revealed to be everything *but compact discs*, obviously an advanced technological form for music presentation. Instead, there are car radios primarily, and when Mia puts on music (for her frenetic dance of 'Girl, You'll be a Woman Soon'), her source is emphasised in close-up as a large tape player, a mode of technology outdated by the new technology of the CD. (It is then an irony of the film's Luddite content and its approach to music that the CD for *Pulp Fiction* has been a giant best-seller.)

Instead, the affinity of *Pulp Fiction* for the cyber-world exhibits itself at levels other than that of the direct representation of new technologies. The connection has to do more with style, feel and structure than with content. As I noted earlier, for example, the websites on Tarantino and *Pulp Fiction* are often marvels of visual and technical sophistication with rich graphics, complicated blends of multimedia presentation and intricate shifts between different modes and sources of information about the films. Now, obviously, many websites on many

subjects exhibit virtuoso composition techniques, but I think it is not
pushing things too far to suggest that *Pulp Fiction* itself displays qualities
that cyber-literate people would respond to particularly well.

In the look of its shots and in the complicated structure of its
narrative(s), *Pulp Fiction* is like an electronic work – a video game or a
story played out on a computer screen. Its images have a baroque
richness, filled up with ever new things to spot, ever new connections to
make (the scenes in Jack Rabbit Slim's are extreme examples of this, in
particular the shot of Vincent moving through the club as so much visual
information is thrown at him and us from the periphery of the frame).
Many of the scenes in *Pulp Fiction* have to do with moving from one
space to the next: from outside the kids' apartment into their living
room; from outside the nightclub into Marsellus's lair; from the hallway
of the boxing venue into the room where Butch's victim lies dead; from
outside Butch's apartment into various rooms; and, especially, from the
upstairs area of the pawnshop down into the dungeon-like area where
Butch discovers the rednecks raping Marsellus. These acts of transition
are often emphasised by insistent movements of the camera (for
example, the tracking shot of Vincent going to meet Marsellus at the
boxing venue). It would not be stretching things too far to suggest that
these highly marked movements from one space to another are not
unlike what happens when, with a click of the mouse, one moves from
one site to the next in a video game or on a website. The scene in which
Butch goes back to rescue Marsellus is certainly like a game, where a
hero arms him or herself before descending into the dungeon to battle
with evil forces.

Like a computer hypertext, where one can jump from one screen
to another, *Pulp Fiction* offers a shifting universe based on disjunction,
substitution, fragmentation. But just as cyber-literate kids appear to have
no trouble in processing the multi-varied, multi-levelled information that
comes rushing at them in cyberspace, so too does a certain class of
spectator have no trouble locking into the formal play of *Pulp Fiction*.
The film-biz journal *Variety* once referred to the new generation of film-
makers like Tarantino, who got their start watching endless hours of

Entering different spaces

rented films on television and working in video stores, as 'Rebels with a pause' (that is, the pause command of the VCR remote control), and it is easy to see in many recent films the structural effects of this form of 'film education'. For example, in *Pulp Fiction*, there is a fascination with interruption and suspension of narrative, with dramatic shifts from one narrative line to another, with variations of speed (like a fast-forward, some scenes bustle forward, while others adopt a pause effect as their dominant tone, as in the silences and dead moments in Mia's night out with Vincent: as she says, 'That's when you know you've found somebody special. When you can just shut the fuck up for a minute, and comfortably share silence.') It seems predictable that the video and DVD of *Pulp Fiction* would prove very successful, since the film invites the repeat viewings, slow-mo analyses, jumps back and forward that are rendered so easy by at-home possession of the film.

Indeed, if earlier I discussed how the cult film experience of a work like *Pulp Fiction* sets up rituals of inclusion and exclusion – the film either resonates for you and does so in intense ways, or it repels you equally intensely – we might well want to make some correlations between the style and structure of the film and a visual literacy that is particular to the cyber-moment of our technologically inflected modernity. If you understand mouse-clicks and web-links and hypertext, you're in the same structural mindset as *Pulp Fiction*, with its disjunctions, its loops of narrative, its dramatic shifts of tone and image. (I remember talking about *Pulp Fiction* to a friend in his mid-forties who is an urban professional but is not cyber-liberate; *Pulp Fiction*, he declared, was a film he just didn't get, didn't understand the interest or appeal of.)

To be sure, there have been many works that eschew simple forward-moving narratives for something more complicated; indeed, in his classic *Mimesis: The Representation of Reality in Western Literature* (1953), critic Eric Auerbach famously began his study of the western literary tradition with an analysis of an extended flashback in *The Odyssey*. What's new is not so much the experiments visible in today's cyber-cinema as the resonances and affective bonds they provoke, often leading the cult film to move out of its netherworld status and into the cinematic mainstream. Whatever their specific representation of technology (or lack thereof), cyber-age films, ranging from *Pulp Fiction* to *The Matrix*, share a number of qualities that encourage the sort of involvement and engagement that we increasingly refer to as 'interactivity': a continuous shifting of tones and transitions between levels that requires constant spectator alertness; an unpredictability of narrative lines that likewise encourages active anticipation and hypothesis-forming; a seductive blurring of the boundaries of illusion and reality (as in the dream sequences of *Pulp Fiction*); images that seduce the eye by their visual richness; likewise, images that are constantly in motion (as in *Pulp Fiction*'s insistent and gliding camera movements); a wise-cracking knowingness that makes audiences feel they're in on a cool joke with the protagonists.

But if stylistic sophistication accounts for much of the appeal of *Pulp Fiction*, so does its reverse: namely, a crudeness or roughness. Earlier, I noted the spelling errors in so many of the websites around Quentin Tarantino and *Pulp Fiction*. While some of this might be a symptom of larger problems of verbal literacy in relation to cyber-literacy, it also seems a phenomenon particular to a figure like Tarantino, where the fan's labour of love frequently appears to have led to a breathless rush to get the amorous declaration out into the world irrespective of its imperfections. Revealingly, the many books that came out on Tarantino after *Pulp Fiction* also typically sport typos and other such errors, this in a realm of publishing where professionalism supposedly is on the lookout for such lapses (my favourite occurs in Jeff Dawson's *Quentin Tarantino: The Cinema of Cool*, which speaks at one point of a potential financier/producer 'who wanted his girlfriend to lay Mr Blonde in *Reservoir Dogs*' when he means 'play').[13]

There is here a blend of the sophisticated and the amateurish (the word 'amateur', we might remember, has etymologically to do with love, 'amour', and the imperfections of the works offered up on the shrine of Tarantino certainly derive from love). This blend finds its corollary in the film itself, where there is a mixture of professionalism and amateurism, of perfection and roughness, of sophistication and awkwardness, of rationalised and rigorous planning and frantic improvisation and moment-to-moment adaptation to new circumstances.

This blend shows up first of all in the very production history of a Tarantino film like *Pulp Fiction*, and the reference to the director is essential, since so much of the film's resonance for its spectator derives from the visibility of its director as much as anything in the film itself. The making of Tarantino films, as we're endlessly told in articles and interviews with the director, involves a mix of complicated calculation (for example, detailed scripts, virtuoso shots and narrative structures designed to wow spectators) *and* joyous game-playing, which is presented as the effortless opposite of work. (One endlessly repeated story has Tarantino and Travolta breaking the ice by playing the *Grease* and the *Welcome Back, Kotter* board games, both of which the director evidently had at his apartment.) With Tarantino, film-making presents itself as both a serious business and as raucous fun, a passionate striving for a good time that one doesn't have to work at. Here, for instance, is Eric Stoltz on being cast as Lance in *Pulp Fiction*, as quoted by Jeff Dawson:

We went to this little Thai restaurant and ate and talked about films. Then we went to his [Tarantino's] apartment and talked about our past girlfriends and how we associated certain films with certain times in our lives and *then* we talked about *Pulp* … After he'd cast the film, he invited us all out to a great Japanese restaurant and we all ate and hung around and told stories. It was a cool feeling. I had a sense then that he'd assembled a wild, wooly bunch. It's really the best way to cast a film … you want a cast and crew that you're gonna want to hang out with and the only way to determine that is to hang out with them.[14]

Pulp Fiction even seems to include a self-referential joke about the tensions between the application of a work ethic in arenas such as film-making and a more slothful world of slacker fun. As film critic Manohla Dargis points out, the scene in which the oh-so professional Winston Wolf has to push Jules and his cohorts to clean up before Jimmie's wife comes home is like a sequence of film direction in which a crew is instructed in the patterns of a *mise en scène*. As Dargis puts it, the scene is

cheerfully self-reflexive, since the orchestration of the purge could easily pass for a crash course in spectacle-making with the Wolf (Harvey Keitel reprising his *Nikita* role) acting as captain of the clean-up and the scene's producer, negotiating the actors and their actions amid the slaughter ('Give me the principals' names again').[15]

No doubt much of the seductiveness that Tarantino holds out for budding film-makers, for example, has to do not only with the films themselves but with the image he offers of film-making: you can make sophisticated works but you can really enjoy yourself while doing it.

But the mix of professionalism and amateurism, and of sophistication and roughness, also shows up in the films themselves and is undoubtedly part of their attraction. For example, *Pulp Fiction* is, on the one hand, filled with professionals whose sophistication is so well honed that it expresses itself as a seductive cool. From the hitmen to the man who cleans up after them to the boss who pulls the strings and gets things done, all without missing a beat, these characters create a confident and controlled cool world. And this prepossessed cool means that its possessor is so in control of things that he or she (but usually he) can incorporate

'I think fast, I talk fast, and I need you guys to act fast if you want to get out of this'

precisely those moments of playfulness, of improvised luxuriating in the moment, that would have seemed the opposite of professionalism. Thus, the hitmen of *Pulp Fiction* can, on the way to their hit, discuss everything from the name for hamburgers in Europe to the notion of TV pilots to the comparative sexual quotient in foot massages versus cunnilingus, and they delay their hit in order to finish their discussion.

On the other hand, except for Winston Wolf, the man who mops up after others, all the professionals of *Pulp Fiction* find their control over their world giving way to chaos. (And Wolf's control is relative. He is after all in Marsellus's employ. Additionally, for all his sophistication and confident cool, Wolf is also shown to be a man who circulates in a

Marsellus in and out of control

world of messy detritus, as we see when he hangs out with a girlfriend at a junk yard.) Endlessly, professionals in *Pulp Fiction* lose their handle on things. For example, as Sharon Willis notes in her essays on *Pulp Fiction*, there is a terrible logic in the film by which the figure who seemingly exerts the greatest control – crime boss Marsellus – is stripped of his authority and made to suffer great iniquity (rape). For much of the film, Marsellus is a disembodied figure (or a partially embodied one, as when we see only the back of his head during his conversation with Butch) who directs others by various means of communication (for example, a cell phone out by his pool). But when Marsellus becomes fully embodied, the accoutrements of power and powerful communication get taken from him and he becomes nothing more than a corporeality, open and vulnerable to the menaces of the world.

Similarly, Jules and Vincent start out as slick, nattily dressed figures of intense cool, only to suffer a degradation of look and attitude that turns them from fashion plates into paragons of grunge: the accidental killing of Marvin covers them in blood and they then have to exchange their chic suits for awkward college T-shirts and bermuda shorts. In passing, it is worth noting that the shirt given to Vincent is from the University of California at Santa Cruz and sports that university's mascot, the Banana Slug: where other universities opt for respectable mascots that often signal athletic might and right, the banana slug connotes a rebellious slothfulness, non-athleticism, an unkempt lack of professionalism.

The very ending of the film draws humour from the transformation of hitmen into geeky beach bums as Jules and Vincent leave the diner in their new outfits trying to maintain as much cool and attitude as they have always had as killers. In fact, in interviews, Tarantino has said that one of the subtexts of *Pulp Fiction* is *Reservoir Dogs*: the intent is to take the professional killers of the earlier film with their sleek, dark, identical suits and then bit by bit besmirch their image of professionalism (although the first film already did this by juxtaposing the confidence before the heist with the bloody and chaotic results after everything has gone wrong).

At first glance, such degrading of professionalism would not seem to be an attraction for viewers, especially the apparently sophisticated

viewer of the cyber-age. But this intimation of the messiness that
underlies all pretence at chic cool has, I would argue, its charms. First of
all, in an age where cyber-work can be done wearing any clothes (for
example, the bathrobe at home), there is a delight in seeing the
uniformed figures of urban professionalism taken down a peg and made
to share in a general condition of grunginess. In the Hollywood that the
hip maverick Tarantino has to deal with, the executives who try to make
all the decisions are referred to as 'suits', and it is perhaps not accidental
that films like *Pulp Fiction* and *Reservoir Dogs* show all the iniquities and
besmirching that can happen to men in suits. A useful account of the
connotations 'suits' hold in the Hollywood world is captured in a *New
York Times* profile of Tarantino actor Tim Roth:

[Roth] becomes unhinged at the sight of a man in a suit. 'It's what the suit
represents – the business world,' he says. 'It's a world I'm not really keen on.
I don't like suits. They bring bad atmosphere. Business people don't know
anything about the arts side of what we're doing.'[16]

Enemy of the State, a film directly inspired by the iconography of
Tarantino films and directed by his buddy Tony Scott, makes clear the
difference between chic professionalism and cyber-geek grunge in its
tension between perfectly groomed military men, who are professional to
the point of being robotic, and computer nerds, who wear grungy old
clothes and seem to be following no authorised rule book.

But if sleek professionalism and messy amateurism seem at first to
be in opposition, there's also a strong sense in which they blur and
intermingle in the cyber-age just as work and play do. What is cool and
what isn't are relative values and each can flip-flop into the other.[17] A
minor moment in *Pulp Fiction* catches the way in which one cannot draw
clear-cut lines in the realm of style and attitude. When Vincent and Jules
trade their suits for the geeky clothes that Jimmie fits them out with, the
latter describes them as looking 'like a couple of dorks', only to be
reminded that they are wearing *his* clothes. Interestingly, the script
version has Jimmie defend himself by a reference to the ways the clothes

make the man – 'I guess you just gotta know how to wear them' – to which Jules replies, 'Yeah, well, our asses ain't the experts on wearin' dorky shit that yours is.' Although it didn't make it into the final cut of the film, this interchange catches how style and coolness can be relativised. You are what you mock, you can become what you felt slickly superior to.

In the cyber-age, indeed, boundaries around professions and professionalism blur. The frontiers, for example, of work and leisure are not so clearly drawn. More people work out of their homes, more hi-tech companies try to incorporate aspects of private life into the firm: for example, loose dress codes; an architecture of relaxation where workers can take a break from work and just hang out; amenities like convenience stores, gyms or running trails. If *Pulp Fiction* incessantly shows professionals who go about their work and will brook no interruption – Jules admonishes both Brad and Marvin to let him conduct his deadly business; Winston Wolf explains to Vincent that he has no time for pleasantries like 'Please' – the film also depicts the lifestyle of grungy layabouts who seem to have nothing to do but do nothing. From the would-be robbers Honey Bunny and Pumpkin, who prefer dangerous ways of getting money over what they consider the horrendous world of 'day jobs', to the (stoned?) kid on the couch Jules will kill in cold professionalism, to bathrobed drug dealer Lance and his hangers-on, who apparently spend their time in front of the TV set (as does the young Butch in his flashback), to the pawnshop redneck who seems to be doing nothing but just hanging around ('The spider just caught a coupla flies', he jubilantly declares when Butch and Marsellus show up as if he's been waiting for ever for a customer or a victim) to Jimmie, who hangs around at home while his wife is at work, *Pulp Fiction* is fascinated by a grubby world of seeming slothfulness that is actually often a way of enjoying and passing time. Lance, in particular, seems the ultimate incarnation of a geek: like a computer nerd, he lives according to a temporality other than that of the 9 to 5 work world (he is up watching TV late at night when Vincent calls to tell him Mia's overdosed); like a number cruncher, he spends much of his time

Slackers

ingesting screen images; he never changes out of the same grungy outfit (a bathrobe) that he makes into his own uniform, his own source of cool (we might contrast this with *Enemy of the State*, where one sign of how far previously slick lawyer Robert Clayton Dean [Will Smith] has been degraded by the government conspiracy around him comes when he has to strip himself of all chic possessions – elegant clothes, plus flashy watch – and escapes in only a bathrobe).

The age of new technology (marked by an aptly named film from 1984, *Revenge of the Nerds*) has certainly seen a coming to power of the nerdy, the geeky, the grungy, the person who by traditional professional standards would seem a slacker but in fact has his or her (but usually his) own way of negotiating the complicated terrain of work and leisure. Grunginess, dorkiness, lack of sophistication become new forms of auratic hipness. (The most famous example obviously is Microsoft's Bill Gates.) Revenge (such as that of the nerds) is often driven by fantasy, and there certainly is a great deal of wish fulfilment in this triumph of a new social type and its representation as sexy (what critic Pat Dowell writing on *Pulp Fiction* refers to as 'geek macho').[18] For example, for all his messiness, Lance is played by the relatively cute Eric Stoltz and gifted with a sexually charged wife (Rosanna Arquette) (she has had a stud put in her tongue because, as she puts it, 'It's a sex thing. It helps fellatio.'). Lance is in his own (grungy) way 'cool'. *Pulp Fiction* participates in a cultural moment where geeky sloppiness itself becomes sexy and stylish, where uncouth becomes a new mode of cool. Note, for instance, how Lance can wisecrack along with the coolest of the cool professionals and make popular culture references just like them. For instance, when challenged by Vincent about the quality of his heroin, Lance defends it with cool confidence: 'My shit, I'll take the Pepsi challenge with Amsterdam shit any ol' time of the fuckin' week.'

This again may be part of the obsession of *Pulp Fiction* for our age. In its blend of perfection and messiness, of professionalism and attractively sloppy amateurism, it enacts and enables new attitudes about labour and leisure, about just what is to be labelled as cool and hip in our society.

'A child was born just the other day' (Harry Chapin)

While one wouldn't want to argue that the seduction of *Pulp Fiction* is just generational, all the elements are there for this film to have special resonance with adolescent boy culture (of the sort one imagines is shared by many of the website designers). We might even say that much of the fascination of *Pulp Fiction* is *infantile*, intending this term less as a judgment than as a description of the world it depicts and the appeal to the spectator that it generates. And it may well be that we have to talk of that appeal as an infantilisation, an active process in which the film reaches out not so much to actual children so much as it constructs all spectators as childlike.

There are perhaps two sides to the infantilism of *Pulp Fiction* and the affect it generates. On the one hand, even as it deals with an adult world of sex, crime and moral decision, the film frequently maintains a tone of wide-eyed innocence, as if characters are seeing from spaces where they can be momentarily free of grown-up responsibility before the inevitable fall into maturity. I've already noted the extent to which the characters frequently look at the world with awe (for example, Vincent at Jack Rabbit Slim's; Butch as he wanders and wonders through the complicated world around him): they are veritable children voyeuristically witnessing the primal scenes of adulthood (for instance, Butch peeking in on the rape of Marsellus). Against this adult world,

'Miserable, violated, and looking like a rag doll'

characters and spectators search for alternative sites of respite, places of non-responsibility where one doesn't have to confront one's own inevitable maturation. Butch, for instance, is a self-infantilising character, luxuriating in the childhood memory of his watch (given to him as he was immersed in the warm womb of children's television) but also fleeing from grown-up violence for the cocoon-like space of his relationship with Fabienne. As the authors of *Tarantino, A to Zed* put it:

For what else is Butch but a big baby? His wide eyes and shaven head mark him thus physically; he shares an exclusive childish language with his babydoll cute paramour Fabienne; piqued, he's prone to fearsome outbursts

Butch as boy and infantile man

of temparament [*sic*], reducing Fabienne to tears; he dreams of himself as a child before the big fight; he keeps less-than-mature souvenirs in his home (his 'little kangaroo' beside the table drawer, for example); hell, he even eats Pop Tarts. His Ordeal in *The Gold Watch* is surely no more than a rite-of-passage from the boy to the man.[19]

Likewise, Fabienne is portrayed as an infantilised figure (and valorised for that, both by Butch and by the film), a saucer-eyed gamine who takes orders from the authoritative male. Butch and Fabienne's discussions of potbellies and blueberry pancakes, the cutesy and sugary way they talk to each other (and the words they use, as when Butch calls her 'sugar pop'),

construct their relationship as a regressive haven from the menaces of the city lurking outside.

If, as I'll suggest in a moment, one manifestation of infantilism shows up in an obsession with a scabrous anality, there is also in *Pulp Fiction* a regressiveness centred on orality. Just as people talk today of the restorative benefits of 'comfort food' – often a mushy cuisine (such as mashed potatoes) that brings one back nostalgically to the succour of childhood – so too does *Pulp Fiction* take solace in food. And this is food not only ingested but lovingly talked about: among others, the food includes fetishising discussions of a variety of hamburgers, french fries

'I have a bit of a tummy, like Madonna when she did "Lucky Star"'

Comfort food

(and their toppings), soft drinks, milkshakes, pancakes, eggs, juice, pie (which we're told by Fabienne is good any time of the day), gourmet coffee, bacon, sausages and pork chops. Food – both its consumption and the spending of time talking about it – becomes a way to slow down the forward movement of the narrative, for people to find leisurely respite before going out again into a cruel, harsh world.

In an adult world of complexity and violence, where characters and spectators try to look on in awe and innocence and build oases of solace, there are sure to be moments where one's safe viewing position is assailed. Butch, for instance, is woken violently from his dream of a childhood spent in front of the television and made to confront his adult decision (not to throw the fight and thereby incur the wrath of Marsellus). And Butch will even more directly have to confront adult issues – violence, responsibility – when he realises that the amulet of his childhood, the watch, has been left behind and he will be forced to venture out into the world after it. Similarly, Vincent is endlessly retreating to the safe, literally anally regressive space of the bathroom, often as a way of fleeing adult decision (should he have an affair with Mia or not?), only to find catastrophe waiting each time he emerges from his haven. The wonderfully sheepish look on Vincent's face when he comes out from the bathroom one last time to find Butch waiting to kill him is a marvellous rendition of the infantilised figure who is caught with 'his pants down'.

But to see Vincent in this moment of vulnerability, and to have him blown away by the blasts of the machine gun, is itself a harsh awakening (especially since, from his television shows and earlier hit movies, John Travolta is for many spectators an object of regressive nostalgia and it is painful to have this character taken away from us). There's something quite cruel – sadistic even – about the ways in which boyish innocence is made to confront the adult world in *Pulp Fiction*.

If, on the one hand, childhood is figured as wide-eyed innocence, the flipside, on the other hand, is indeed sadistic cruelty. Comparing their own inadequacies to the adult world around them, children seek mastery, and often the only way for this to manifest itself is in nastiness, aggressivity, downright brattiness. As much as it hopes for sweet 'grace' (the name of the chopper that Butch and Fabienne ride off on after his run-ins with the violent world), *Pulp Fiction* also luxuriates in what adults disparagingly refer to in young people as 'adolescent behaviour'.

There are many manifestations in the film of this smirky, bratty infantilism. First of all, there is the sheer fascination with anality, like that of little kids caught up in jokes about the butt: so many scenes in bathrooms, so many references to buttocks and terrible things that can be done to them (as in Marsellus's famous line, 'I'm gonna git Medieval on your ass'). The speech by Captain Koons about the gold watch that has been passed down to Butch by generations of fathers directly uses anality to shock and veer the narrative into unexpected territory. Starting off in serious directions (although perhaps already skewed in a weird direction by Walken's performance, since he is always an eccentric presence on screen), the speech quickly becomes the virtual equivalent of gross-out humour as we learn about all the men who, in the script's words, 'hid this uncomfortable hunk of metal up [the] ass'.

Connected to the relentless anality in *Pulp Fiction*, there is a fascination in the film for the secretion of bodily fluids – for example, what the script refers to as the 'blood and puke' all over Mia when she overdoses, or the brain and blood that are spread all over the car when Vincent accidentally shoots Marvin. Not for nothing does the film treat

'He hid it in the one place he knew he could hide somethin''

Marvin's death as a high moment of gross-out comedy, for it is working in the world of infantile humour. As Sharon Willis notes, bodily secretions erupt in the films in ways that approximate childhood obsession with smearing (think, for instance, of little kids with finger paints):

As [*Reservoir Dogs*] progresses, more and more blood drains out of Orange, until he writhes and struggles and slides around in what looks more and more like a spill of red paint. Consequently, this blood seems to signify something other than the violence that produces it, and to refer more definitively to the shocking aesthetic effects the smears of red on white

'Fucked up repugnant shit'

background produce – a violent soiling … In a central and particularly
hilarious moment [in *Pulp Fiction*], Jules, clearly the film's best cleaner, as
well as its most articulate speaker, is infuriated by Vince's poor bathroom
habit, since he leaves the washcloth stained with blood, and looking like a
'maxi-pad'. This sequence is about hygiene in an uproarious way; but its
structural link between blood and the bathroom suggests that blood is
Tarantino's way of 'smearing.' Soiling and cleaning, then, become central
organizing processes for these films – at the literal and figurative levels.[20]

A secondary and complementary form of infantilism in *Pulp Fiction*
manifests itself in the film's sheer amusement in flaunting exhibitions of
bad taste. Not merely does the film deal with smearing, but it seems to
luxuriate in it (just as *Reservoir Dogs* seems fascinated by its outpouring
of blood). From Jules's double-take repulsion at the idea of the Dutch
eating fries with mayonnaise to the sheer revulsion he experiences for the
job of cleaning up the blood-and-brain soaked car (as he puts it, 'This is
some fucked up repugnant shit!'), *Pulp Fiction* is vivid and visceral in the
ways it gleefully catalogues things that inspire disgust in both its
characters and its audience. And we might take this idea of 'inspiration'
literally, for, like gross-out humour, *Pulp Fiction* assumes that the
sparking of disgust can be a delightful, invigorating activity. Like kids
who are both attracted to and claim to be put off by that which is
'yucky', the film flirts with an abject messiness that both repels and
attracts with the dialectic of the sick joke.

And like such jokes, which challenge us to see how far we will follow
before we are grossed-out, *Pulp Fiction* plays with the limits of what is
acceptable, what will be too much. The whole of Butch's run-in with
Marsellus and then with the rednecks seems caught up in a wacky spiral of
bad-taste one-upmanship – how will each moment top the previous one
for visceral weirdness? – and the audience is made to play along with a
spectacle of excess and of escalation (as when Butch keeps trading
weapons of revenge for ones that are bigger and more destructive). If a
sugary side to *Pulp Fiction* depicts a doe-like wide-eyed innocence that
looks on in sheepish awe, there is also in the film a more aggressive

voyeurism that peers in on freakish things in order to be inspired by them. For example, when Lance and Vincent get ready to plunge a giant needle into the overdosed Mia to try to save her, Lance's wife Jody hovers gleefully in the background – her face 'alive with anticipation', as the screenplay instructs – and reacts to Mia's violent reawakening by chortling with delight, 'That was fucking trippy!' (something many members of the audience may also be feeling at that moment).

An additional manifestation of infantile behaviour shows up in *Pulp Fiction*'s fascination with obscenity. I'll come back shortly to debates about the racial implications of the film's obsession with one particular obscenity – 'nigger'. The racial epithet carries a particular social import. But in *Pulp Fiction*, it takes place also among a slew of obscenities (and strings of obscenities combined in fanciful fashion) that are used for brute, visceral shock value. Here, again, we can refer back to the film-making process behind Quentin Tarantino's films, with its emphasis on 'having a good time': as one watches *Pulp Fiction* or reads through the screenplay, one can't help but feel that the film-making team (the screenwriter-director, the actors) is enjoying the game of seeing just how many obscenities it can pepper the film with (and just how imaginative and colourful its epithets can be). Like little kids learning the new words of bad language and then flaunting their new power by chanting the words over and over again (even if they don't completely know what they mean), *Pulp Fiction* deliberately wallows in its obscenity by pouring on the tastelessness as if there are no limits. Like little children who delight in repeating forbidden words when out of adult range, *Pulp Fiction* uses the relatively safe space of an unreal movie about unreal characters to engage in a rush of vulgarity, bad taste, bathroom humour and gross-out display.

In fact, the role of limits and boundaries – and what happens when they are not enforced – is central to *Pulp Fiction*'s flirtation with adolescent or infantile fantasy. I've already suggested that, especially in the Mia overdose scene and the 'The Bonnie Situation' episode, the film resembles a TV sitcom with the protagonists scurrying to clean up a mess before the authority figure arrives home. Like little kids, the central characters either follow parental authority slavishly (the hitmen are in thrall to big Marsellus, the puller of strings, the giver and taker of life) or try to hide their messy foul-ups from that authority (Butch pulling a scam on Marsellus, Vincent covering up Mia's overdose, the guys trying to clean up blood-and-brains before Bonnie gets home). 'The Bonnie Situation', in particular, seems to capture an infantile world in which a bunch of cool guys are reduced to veritable little children fearing the mommy who might come home and discover how they've smeared their mess all over her domestic space. As Tarantino puts it in an interview, speaking of the criminals in *Pulp Fiction*:

They're a cross between criminals and actors and children playing roles … It was never a conscious decision, playing on the idea of big men are actually little boys with real guns, but it kept coming out and I realized as I wrote *Pulp*, that actually fits. You can even make the analogy with the scene with Jules and Vincent at Jimmie's house, they're afraid of their mom coming home. You spilled shit on the carpet – clean up the mess you made from screwing around before your mom gets home.[21]

Revealingly, and as I pointed out earlier, Bonnie's husband, Jimmie, is played by Tarantino himself, and his character, although relatively minor, condenses much of the ambivalence the film depicts about the borders between adult malehood and a regressive infantile state. On the one hand, Jimmie is a figure who at first refuses to play along with the boys and reminds them of responsibility (as he says, 'Make your phone calls, talk to your people, and then get the fuck out of my house'). Indeed, if *Pulp Fiction*, with its crises, can remind one of the structure of TV, Jimmie is like a character who refuses the televisual world: when Jules tries to calm Jimmie down by turning their dialogue into a veritable TV commercial where one person discovers the wonders of a product a friend has sprung on him/her, Jimmie refuses to play along:

JULES [drinking coffee that Jimmie has prepared]: Goddam, Jimmie, this is some serious gourmet shit. Me an' Vincent woulda been satisfied with freeze-dried Tasters Choice. You spring this gourmet fuckin' shit on us. What flavour is this?

JIMMIE: Knock it off, Julie.

JULES: What?

JIMMIE: I'm not a cob of corn, so you can stop butterin' me up. I don't need you to tell me how good my coffee is. I'm the one who buys it, I know how fuckin' good it is. When Bonnie goes shoppin', she buys shit. I buy the gourmet expensive shit, 'cause when I drink it, I wanna taste it. But what's on my mind at the moment isn't the coffee in my kitchen, it's the dead nigger in my garage.

On the other hand, if he tries to be a mature boss, Jimmie in fact shares many of the characteristics of infantile regression: he's whiny, he's petulant, he looks on with wide-eyed awe as others go about their business, he is in thrall to powers of authority. (For example, when Winston Wolf offers him money from the imperious Marsellus, Jimmie readily goes along with the plans; significantly, Wolf has set Jimmie down on the bed and speaks to him of 'Uncle Marsellus' as if he were lecturing a little child on the ways of the adult world.) Above all, Jimmie is a figure over-associated with the outpouring of obscenity that runs through the film and expresses a childlike obsession with defying the rules of propriety.

Jimmie in the bedroom

'It don't matter if you're black or white' (Michael Jackson)

Earlier, I noted that we need to distinguish in the flood of obscenity in *Pulp Fiction* the potentially unique role that racial epithet plays within it. In fact, Jimmie is, of the white characters, the one who says 'Nigger' the most. (Just for the record, Vincent, Butch and Mia never say it; Lance says it once; one of the rednecks says it once; Jimmie says it three times). It is the African-American characters who use the epithet in the film on a widespread basis.

In having his own character repeatedly employ a racial obscenity in interchanges with an African-American character who also uses the same word regularly, Tarantino seems first of all to be engaging once again in boyish fun, a sense of empowered liberation in which one gleefully flaunts the rules. One senses that above all Tarantino fills his film with outrageous behaviour (including racial attitude) because he can do so, because no one will stop him. Indeed, an oft-repeated story about Tarantino's visit to the National Film Theatre recounts how a black man in the audience angrily said that the director couldn't get away with using 'nigger', to which Tarantino calmly replied, 'I do'. In passing, though, we might note that Samuel L. Jackson himself has expressed reservations about the racial politics of Tarantino's cameo. As an interview in the *Observer* recounts:

Jackson estimates that Tarantino has a '95 per cent' ear for African-American language, but feels he got it wrong in his cameo in *Pulp Fiction*. 'The only time I had an issue was when he had to say "dead nigga storage",' recalls Jackson. 'I kept saying: "Quentin, as long as you say 'nigger,' it's going to be like fingernails on a chalkboard. You've got to say 'N-I-G-G-A-H, nigga.' That means you're familiar with the use of the word and you've used it in mixed company, not just with some white guys'".[22]

It might be argued that in having racial epithets used by characters who do not otherwise seem racist (with the exception of the rednecks, who clearly inhabit a different moral universe from virtually everyone else in the film), *Pulp Fiction* may less be trying to say that there's more racism here than we had first assumed than attempting to picture racial reference as one more form of the admirable cool behaviour that gains men recognition throughout the Tarantino universe. Tarantino films appropriate a black aesthetic as they look back to the 70s and find in its popular culture a fount of attractive coolness. The appropriated aesthetics of black cool show up in *Pulp Fiction* in a number of borrowings: from music (and in using music as a riff from which one builds complicated new structures); from blaxploitation cinema; from language itself (slang, linguistic codes of inclusion and exclusion); from fashion and style; from, more generally, the assumption of a mode of being and of performing the codes of everyday life that takes coolness – the seductive ability to maintain slick calm under pressure – as a positive virtue.

That racial difference can be construed as an enviable source of cool has its own ideological problems – what does it mean to appropriate another culture? – but it is a different stance than one that imputes inferiority. In an article on 'Quentin Tarantino's Negro Problem', Devon Jackson outlines the difficulties of this position of envying appropriation of African-American style:

In an age in which so many white men of all classes perceive a loss of racial superiority and economic opportunity, perhaps the most alluring of vicarious role models are the gangsta rappers and b-ball megastars. ... In [Tarantino's] world, blacks are the epitome of cool; as are their language and style; hence, 'nigga' is a cool word. Put all of the above into the character who is white and that white person becomes ultracool. Ain't nothin' cooler than niggas, 'cept maybe a white guy who knows the whole nigga scene and how to mingle with them. It's Mailer's tired old 'White Negro' thing all over again.[23]

To be sure, such envy can easily turn into a violent jealousy that wants to see the initially admired Other demeaned and debased. For instance, as I've noted earlier, one narrative line of the film has to do with the humbling of a black man (and his salvation by a white): Marsellus is established initially as a figure who incarnates power (but in a

Cool

disembodied way: he is a voice, a telephone call, a man who is dangerous even when he's out of town, as Vincent knows only too well when he takes Mia out). But when Butch betrays Marsellus by refusing to throw the fight, it's as if this first challenge to authority gives momentum to an increasing vulnerability on Marsellus's part. Where early scenes had given Marsellus an aura by imaging him only in veiled ways, the first time we see him fully corporealised is at the moment when Butch will run him over and initiate the sequence of events that leads to Marsellus being raped by the rednecks. In the words of black feminist critic bell hooks:

Note that even when the black male arrives at the top, as Marsellus does in *Pulp Fiction* – complete with a lying, cheating lapdog white child-woman wife – he is unmasked as only an imitation cowboy, not the real thing. And in case viewers haven't figured out that Marsellus ain't got what it takes, the film turns him into a welfare case – another needy victim who must ultimately rely on the kindness of strangers (i.e. Butch, the neoprimitive white colonizer, another modern-day Tarzan) to rescue him from the rape-in-progress that is his symbolic castration, his return to the jungle, to a lower rung on the food chain.[24]

Marsellus lives the rape as an intensely shameful experience but one that he must then attempt to control. As he orders Butch after the rednecks have been dispatched:

Power through veiling

Two things I ask: don't tell nobody about this. This shit's between me and you and the soon-to-be-livin'-the-rest-of-his-short-ass-life-in-agonising-pain, Mr Rapist here. It ain't nobody else's business. Two: leave town. Right now. And when you're gone, stay gone.

But to say that the film depicts the humiliation of Marsellus is not to say it endorses it. Certainly, the scene of rape is not handled with the jokey and gleeful relish that other acts of violence receive in the film. The rapists are clearly among the lowest figures depicted in the film; if anything, it might be more appropriate to find the scene less an example of racism than perhaps of classism and implicit homophobia, the worst thing that can befall a manly man being revealed to be anal penetration by another man. Again, as Devon Jackson puts it, by entering into the logic of the film:

[L]et's call a spade a spade: the pawn shop scene reeks of homophobia. Sure, the two white rapists exhibit no obviously 'homosexual' mannerisms, but just because they are sadistic rednecks does not exclude them from being homosexual. ... These two faggots are deviants of the worst kind: queers who pass themselves off as he-men. They are thus more fearsome, vengeance taken upon them for their grotesque sins shall be meted out twice as harsh. So Willis going back to save Rhames has nothing to do with loyalty and everything to do with the bond among heterosexual men that says: male viewers, fret not, for I shall send Butch back into the bowels of that faggot hellhole for a most necessary, most logical *Death Wish/Deliverance*-style retribution. Yes, Marsellus is my foe, but I respect his bigness, his cool, his niggerness.[25]

In any case, whatever vulnerability Marsellus displays is one he quickly overcomes. Once the rednecks have been routed, he may announce to Butch, 'I'm pretty fuckin' far from okay!,' but it is evident that Marsellus will be re-establishing his power over the world. (Interestingly, in the script the scene in the pawnshop ends with Marsellus enlisting the help of Winston Wolf; once again, Marsellus is the man who commands by pulling the strings at a distance.) As when he is run over by Butch, yet rises up 'from the dead' to engage in aggressive pursuit, Marsellus comes back resiliently from the iniquity perpetrated on him in the pawnshop and quickly regains his manly poise. The last image we see of him is not that different from the first time he appeared in the film: viewed from behind, Marsellus is a massive figure of power who signals goodbye to Butch with a calculated flick of the hand that indicates he is still a figure of cool control and resolve.

Pulp Fiction rarely wavers in its admiration for things black. The use of racial epithets is a manifestation of this admiration. Whatever political problems we would want to find in this process of co-optation have to be examined as something other than easy racism. We might, for instance, want to take to heart the reservation expressed in an otherwise favourable commentary on Tarantino in the *Sunday Telegraph*:

The whole project of [*Jackie Brown*] gives off the desperate air of a dorky white boy who wants to be black. Perhaps all Tarantino's work is minstrelsy: as much as the 19th-century Christy Minstrels rubbing burnt cork on their faces for the amusement of middle-class whites, movie violence is about appropriating real pain and transforming it into a vaudeville turn. Tarantino is the master, the greatest poseur in a poseur's culture.[26]

Jackie Brown

'Every day, I write the book' (Elvis Costello)

Significantly, as with the websites, much of the writing on Tarantino and on *Pulp Fiction* is also caught up in structures of obsession, sacrificing supposed scholarly objectivity for passionate involvement. (And, as we've seen, this is true even of writings that set out to take a critical distance from Tarantino. For example, Robin Wood's virulent attack on *Pulp Fiction* comes, as he tells us, from the need, in his words, to 'loudly' defend another film, Greg Araki's *The Doom Generation*, against association with Tarantino's film.)

As with the massive outpouring of websites, there is a relatively large number of books dedicated to Quentin Tarantino. In English alone, there are six, quite a significant number for a director with only three films to his credit (and, in fact, almost all the books came out after *Pulp Fiction*, the second film, as if that was the work that crystallised the obsessive need to write about this director). Significantly, none of the books are scholarly studies and all present themselves more as works of fandom that try to invoke the feel and cool atmosphere of the Tarantino films that I've outlined above. Even many of the titles resonate with admiration: *King Pulp: The Wild World of Quentin Tarantino*; *Quentin Tarantino: The Cinema of Cool*; *Quentin Tarantino: Shooting from the Hip*.

As with the websites, what is most striking about the many books is their repetition. I've already mentioned how the books share (among themselves and with the websites) a certain sloppy attitude toward spelling and literacy; these, again, are works of amateurism (from within the professional world of publishing). And there are other repetitions. For example, several share the same photos (even to the extent of using the same cover images). Above all, there is a repetition of information – of anecdotes and legends, especially – as if there is an established knowledge on Tarantino and his films that allows for endless re-citation (just as the films themselves recycle elements of previous popular culture). Even the primary French book on Tarantino (Jean-Pierre Deloux's *Quentin Tarantino ... fils de pulp* [child of pulp]) retells the same stories. Interestingly, for all their repetition, each new book announces itself as having discovered the truth that previous books missed. In this world of fandom, there is both a creation of community (everyone shares in the obsessive love for the object of admiration) and fierce competition (each fan wants his or her love to be the special one; as Kathy Bates says in *Misery* to the beloved writer she will trap in her house, 'I'm your biggest fan').

The fact that a director with so few films gets so much attention is itself revealing. In particular, it is notable that it is *Pulp Fiction* that should have encouraged this flurry of writing. The film seems to have served as a rallying point for a heavily emotionally invested taste culture that had to celebrate the emergence of a new cool voice. By the act of celebration, the culture could feel that it was part of that emergence and that a little bit of the love it shone on its object of veneration was turned back onto itself. Many of the books seem to pride themselves on having got close to Tarantino and shared in his aura (Wensley Clarkson, for instance, reproduces a picture with the caption, 'Author Wensley Clarkson and Quentin share a joke during a Horror convention in Los Angeles in May 1995'; it's also interesting to note how much fan writing on Tarantino refers to him as 'QT' or just 'Quentin', as if participating in structures of intimacy).

Within the world of cinema, there are few other cases in which a film-maker has received so much attention so early on in his or her career. In fact, it may well be that the appropriate comparison is not to film-makers (people who stay behind the scene and create works that are supposed to speak for themselves) but to media performers (singers, comedians, actors, celebrities of any sort), who put their own bodies and personae into play and into the spotlight.

One comparison that does pop up from the film-making world is to Orson Welles and his own early success (*Citizen Kane* by the age of twenty-six). Jean-Pierre Deloux puts it this way:

[Tarantino] has instinct, an instinct tempered by a skill at composition and an intelligence of movement, a beautiful freedom in scripting which refers back to that other wonder boy of the cinema, Orson Welles, whose genius inaugurated the second half-century of the cinematograph's existence.

Certainly, there is an (enormous) step to mount between *Citizen Kane* and *Reservoir Dogs*; it is no less the case that *Reservoir Dogs* marks out a path to follow as well as giving witness to the tone of the age. It is not for nothing that in the past, Orson Welles was the only young film-maker to unleash such outpouring among spectators, while instigating the recognition of cinema as a major art, and no longer as a simple diversion.[27]

One could no doubt find points of comparison between the films of Welles and Tarantino: two 'boy wonders' who not only display an artistic ambition to use rigour and seriousness to make of cinema an art but also a boyish desire just to have fun (according to legend, when he first went on the set, Welles said that it was like getting the biggest toy train for Christmas); a related, flashy desire to show off cinematic technique to dazzle the spectator; a concomitant concern with complicated forms of narrativity (the complex temporality of *Citizen Kane* and *Pulp Fiction*); consequentially, a certain relativisation of knowledge, as no one perspective is held to reveal the complete truth about a particular situation or life in general (the ambiguities in the accounts of Charles Foster Kane, the multiple versions of the heist in *Jackie Brown*); a fascination with baroque images (and narrative lines) in which the eye wanders around a visually rich space (for example, Xanadu in *Citizen Kane*, Jack Rabbit Slim's in *Pulp Fiction*); connected to this, a sense of camera movement as a penetration into a special world (the entry into Xanadu at the beginning of *Citizen Kane*, the numerous transitions into new spaces that I've outlined in *Pulp Fiction*). In particular, Welles and Tarantino are directors of obsession, creating and depicting worlds apart peopled by special characters who set themselves off from ordinary society and try to live by personal or private codes or rules. And like Welles with the elegiac *Magnificent Ambersons*, Tarantino follows up flashy and youthfully exuberant debut work with a more autumnal, nostalgic effort (*Jackie Brown*) that coincides with a relative diminishing of celebrity and media attention.

For Michael Denning, in his book *The Cultural Front: The Laboring of American Culture in the Twentieth Century*, Welles was one of the first great multimedia stars in America, putting his own persona into an array of cultural forms from radio and dramatic theatre to vaudeville (his magic acts) from popular journalism to cinema (and later television).[28] With the release of *Pulp Fiction*, Tarantino tries to take a clear place in this lineage of celebrity-artists, appearing endlessly on talk shows and in cameo roles in movies, becoming an inevitable presence in the mass media. As Deloux says at the end of his Welles–Tarantino comparison, having spoken of the earlier fan outpouring for Welles, 'The contemporary public has not erred. It celebrates Youth through Quentin Tarantino, and this is perhaps a first for Hollywood with the exception perhaps of James Dean who was in fact not a director, but a sort of Rock Star.'[29]

Here, in fact, it might be necessary to nuance the comparison with Welles. What Deloux refers to as an outpouring of fandom for Welles is perhaps overstated (*Citizen Kane*, for instance, did not do well beyond a few urban venues, and *The Magnificent Ambersons* was a bomb). Much of the attention given to Welles as a director can be explained from the fact that he was already a well-known celebrity (especially for his infamous *War of the Worlds* broadcast), whom people followed less as fans than as curious onlookers waiting to see if he would stumble or not. In contrast, Tarantino came to cinema as an unknown figure, who then quickly gained both celebrity and the obsessive fan pressures that come with it (only after his first films did people ask if he would also stumble and prove, à la F. Scott Fitzgerald's declaration in his Hollywood novel, *The Last Tycoon*, 'There are no second acts in American lives'). Indeed, a vast majority of the numerous articles on Tarantino in the three-year hiatus between *Pulp Fiction* and *Jackie Brown* endlessly wonder if Tarantino still 'has it' and pore over various incidents to see if they are signs of a fall (for example, a Tarantino brawl in a restaurant; a surfeit of media appearances that threaten to become irritating; tensions between the director and members of his film-making family; a series of acting appearances that garner more criticism than praise; the sheer length of the hiatus itself). If, in Denning's argument, Welles is an important early celebrity in media culture, Tarantino takes that tradition to an extreme. It is not accidental that, in contrast to the literature on Tarantino, most of the books on Welles are serious biographies or rigorous scholarly studies that came out long after the fact of his meteoric rise, as if distance and time help mute obsessive, unquestioning fandom.

But for all their fan-culture exuberance and exaggeration, and given their endless recycling of the same anecdotes, the books on Tarantino do allow us to construct a narrative of *Pulp Fiction*'s production. Here's the story as pieced together from the books (and confirmed, as much as possible, from published interviews and trade journal articles):

In 1992, after the breakthrough success of *Reservoir Dogs*, Tarantino hung out in Amsterdam to write the script for his next film. Originally, *Reservoir Dogs* seems to have been part of the script idea for *Pulp Fiction* but it had split off into a full story of its own. Some of the ideas that went into the script came from friend Roger Avary (who had been a co-worker at the famous Video Archives store where Tarantino had worked and honed his cinephilia). Avary had written the segment that eventually became Butch's gold watch story, and he had expanded it into a feature film script called *Pandemonium Reigns*. Tarantino bought back the script and reduced it back into a section of *Pulp Fiction*. But later on, there would be ambiguities over credits: at the Golden Globe Awards, for example, only Tarantino was named as best screenwriter, but at the Academy Awards, Tarantino and Avary shared the Oscar. The actual credits on the film state 'Written and directed by Quentin Tarantino. Story by Quentin Tarantino and Roger Avary.'

Once the script for *Pulp Fiction* was completed, Tarantino and his producer buddy Lawrence Bender took it to Jersey Films (co-run by Stacey Sher, Michael Shamberg and Danny DeVito), which had offered Tarantino close to a million dollars for a script. Tarantino and Bender's company, A Band Apart, had negotiated a deal with Jersey that involved an offer of initial financing plus office facilities in exchange for partnership in the film and permission to shop the script to a studio. Jersey took it to TriStar Films, which had a first-look option on Jersey films. The company decided to pass on producing *Pulp Fiction*: the rumour is that the studio heads were bothered by the violence and scenes in which the John Travolta character shoots up heroin. But a piece in the *Los Angeles Times* contemporaneous with the pre-production phase of *Pulp Fiction* has another interpretation:

TriStar pictures is insisting that Jersey Films co-chairmen Danny De Vito and Michael Shamberg shouldn't be paranoid or take it personally that the studio isn't going to make yet another of their planned movies, writer-director Quentin Tarantino's new dark comedy *Pulp Fiction* ... TriStar apparently got cold feet and decided not to go forward with production this fall because they feared it could be hard to market. The studio's nose-thumbing at both *Pulp Fiction*, an under-$10 million movie, and *Reality Bites*, another low-cost production, don't appear to be unrelated events. A source at the studio explained that TriStar is currently looking to make and release more higher profile, bigger-budgeted mainstream movies with stars and at this point has little interest in more offbeat fare, even if the financial risks are lower.[30]

Luckily, another company, Miramax, which had bought the US distribution rights for *Reservoir Dogs* and made lots of money from that experience, agreed to finance *Pulp Fiction*. In fact, it was the first film that Miramax (which had recently become a Disney subsidiary) financed entirely. Tarantino was given the same scriptwriting fee that he had been promised at TriStar, and the film went into an eight-week shoot with a budget of $8.5 million. The largest part of the budget went to building the Jack Rabbit Slim's set (but some savings were made by having the production offices at the same site so as to cut down on transportation costs). Something else that also helped keep costs down was a plan that Lawrence Bender devised in which all the main actors were paid the same amount, rather than according to a hierarchy of celebrity and importance.

Some of the casting history for the film is quite intriguing. For example, there was evidently some thought of giving the role of Vincent Vega to Michael Madsen (who plays Vic Vega in *Reservoir Dogs*, leading to speculation – especially in the websites – that Vincent is Vic's brother in the continuous Tarantino narrative universe). There was also talk of Daniel Day-Lewis playing the part. Similarly, there was some competition for the character of co-hitman Jules, with Laurence Fishburne also testing for the role. A number of other actresses were also suggested for the Mia character: for example, Meg Ryan, Meg Tilly, Holly Hunter, Brigitte Nielsen, Rosanna Arquette (who ends up as Lance's wife in the film) and Alfre Woodard (which would certainly have changed the racial significance of the Mia–Marsellus marriage). And a recurrent story has Pam Grier (later the star of *Jackie Brown*) originally being considered for the role of Lance's wife.

Production began on 20 September 1993. In May 1994, *Pulp Fiction* had its première at the Cannes Film Festival and won the highest prize, the Palme d'Or, from a jury presided over by Clint Eastwood. This success encouraged Miramax to give the film a big publicity push, which included opening it in over 1,200 theatres across the United States. Nominated for seven Oscars (Best Picture, Best Director, Best Actor [Travolta], Best Supporting Actor [Jackson], Best Supporting Actress [Thurman], Best Original Screenplay and Best Editing), it won for Best Original Screenplay. Eventually, it made well over $200 million at the box office (and the CD and published script for the film were also big sellers).

'Turn off your mind, relax, and flow downstream' (The Beatles)

If *Pulp Fiction* were merely the obsessive fantasy of a subculture of geeks, slackers and would-be cool sophistos, it might be easy to see the phenomena of the film as just an eccentricity, one more case of the ways historical moments generate curious fringes, strange epiphenomena. But it is apparent that *Pulp Fiction* confounds by moving from the margins into the mainstream: an independent film that ends up a big box-office success and major award-winner, an experiment with narrative structure that becomes eminently watchable. The film seems central to its age.

It becomes necessary, then, to assess not only the immediate fancult around *Pulp Fiction* but also the film's larger place in its culture (some of which we can establish by understanding fan culture as a subculture whose very existence says things about the culture at large).

Typically, *Pulp Fiction* is seen as a key work of popular *post-modernism*. But to treat the film this way depends on what one means by 'post-modern'. Moreover, if one wants to make the case that the film does indeed come under some characterisation of post-modernity, it is still necessary then to ask another question – what is accomplished by treating it as a post-modern work? This then leads to perhaps the most important question of all: whatever *Pulp Fiction* is, how typical is it of contemporary American film production or, even more generally, of trends in contemporary American culture *per se* (which may be another way of asking whether post-modernism is indeed the dominant cultural trend of our moment or only one force among several)?

The question of post-modernity is a complicated one and has given rise to a massive literature of explication (including dozens of guidebooks, each with its own take on the matter). Certainly, in many of the writings, *Pulp Fiction* is cited as a major example of post-modern tendencies in contemporary culture. It's even treated as an automatic, evident, inevitable reference in the literature. One of the most curious examples of this appears on the cover of an issue of the *London Review of Books*, which announces a piece by traditionalist literary critic David Bromwich entitled, very directly, 'Tarantinisation'. But the reader who expects a discussion of director Quentin Tarantino is – initially, at least – in for a surprise: Bromwich's work is in fact not a discussion of Tarantino at all but a review-essay of Marxist scholar Fredric Jameson's *The Cultural Turn: Selected Writings on Postmodernism* and Perry Anderson's *The Origins of Postmodernity* (a history of the concept which is also a gloss on Jameson's book), while the only reference to Tarantino (a vague one at that) is a quotation from Anderson on the 'disneyfication of protocols and tarantinisation of practices' in the age of post-modernity.

That 'Tarantino' can become an automatic noun to describe broad (post-modern) processes at work in social life today seems intensely revealing, suggesting that in some major way, even for writers who don't think much of Tarantino's cinema, his films do capture the tone, the feel, the style of our contemporaneity.

At first sight, the parallel Perry Anderson draws between Tarantino and Disney, given the violence of the former and the feel-good family values approach of the latter, might seem paradoxical and quite curious (despite the fact that Disney was the parent organisation for *Pulp Fiction* producer Miramax). Tarantino seems to thrust us into a grungy world of violence that is anathema to Disney ideology (the messiness of Tarantino's world would seem to be the opposite of the purity of Disneyland where, for example, trash is supposed to disappear mysteriously in under a minute). But we can find connections.

Disneyfication might suggest, first of all, the global spread of a particularly artificial lifestyle (not just through entertainment products but now also throughly planned communities like the Disney-sponsored Celebration small-town experience in Florida). Such theme parks and planned communities pull away from ordinary experience, creating, virtually, an alternative universe (which sometimes is a cleaned up, sugar-powdered version of the universe we live in). Similarly, in a film like *Pulp Fiction*, as we have already seen, there is an emphasis on special ways of life and of special sites where those lives can be played out. *Pulp Fiction* frequently projects a world apart – nightclubs and post-modern restaurants, homes of rich gangsters, weird chambers of redneck torture – peopled by special figures (most notably, the possessors of cool) who have created their own rules and rituals (just as the visitor to a theme park is supposed to leave certain worldly thoughts and pressures behind).

Despite several scenes on everyday city streets where ordinary people can get caught up in the violence of the special figures (as when Marsellus shoots at Butch and hits instead an anonymous bystander), *Pulp Fiction* seems to take place in a parallel universe, one in which many of the rules of our everyday life are suspended. In fact, the point of the scene with the bystanders is that they are precisely that: inconsequential characters who don't really figure in any substantial way in the separate universe of the film's special people and who can only look on, get in the way, and then get passed over as the story continues on its exaggerated, unreal way. (Significantly, when Marsellus recovers consciousness on one such city street after being run over by Butch, the passers-by who offer him aid are all women – a relatively unimportant gender in *Pulp Fiction*'s concern with *mano-à-mano* competition.) Central to the film is its fascination for made-up spaces, cartoon-like built environments. Spaces here are built by the characters, who create self-contained worlds that reflect their personal style and obsession, as in Lance's popular-culture-filled house/haven, but they are built also by the film-makers, who construct an artificial universe for the characters to move around in. For example, far more typical of the film than its few glimpses of real city streets is the way it depicts the taxi-cab ride with cabby Esmarelda that Butch takes to reach his safe haven with Fabienne. The scene is filmed with a deliberately fake-looking rear projection that renders the journey unreal, ethereal even. Similarly, after Vincent shoots up heroin at the beginning of his strange night out with Mia, his drive to her house is presented with rear projection and turns the journey into an ethereal voyage into another dimension.

Indeed, although we would probably classify *Pulp Fiction* within urban-realism crime-related genres such as film noir, the film seems to partake as well of genres and filmic forms devoted to creating imaginary worlds and artificial environments. As Amanda Lipman puts it in a review of the film, 'Like *Reservoir Dogs*, [*Pulp Fiction*] is stylistically shot in neo-cartoon style, with massive, distorting close-ups offset by attractively angled shots. The effect again is of a hard, closed, rather linear world.'[31] There is, in fact, a fair amount of the look and feel of the animated cartoon in *Pulp Fiction*: exaggerated characters at the edge of caricature (for example, the massive and bald-headed Marsellus); vibrantly bright colours that seem to shimmer off the screen (as in the

Deliberately fake background

Jack Rabbit Slim's scene and the sharp black-and-white contrasts of Mia and her home); sharp angles and boldly composed shots that call attention to themselves like the strongly dramatic framings in a cartoon or comic-strip panel; wild situations in which real-life rules seem suspended; an extreme violence that is simultaneously explosive and banal (for example, like a cartoon character who endlessly gets blown up, Marsellus rebounds from his car accident and goes loping after Butch). Like a cartoon, *Pulp Fiction* has us participate in the creation of an imaginary world in which figures are called into life only for the duration of the fiction they are part of (note how much of the film is about characters popping up and then disappearing – for example, Winston Wolf, who turns up miraculously to save the day). Vincent's description of the simulacrum that is Jack Rabbit Slim's could also be a description of the ways *Pulp Fiction* simulates and makes manifest the fictional nature of that simulation: to use Vincent's phrase, Slim's and *Pulp Fiction* are both 'like a wax museum with a pulse rate'.

Pulp Fiction even refers directly to the cartoon's transportation and translation of the real world into artificiality in a scene that takes place outside Jack Rabbit Slim's. Mia responds to Vincent's unwillingness to go in by indicating he should not be a 'square'. She moves her fingers in the shape of a square and, as she does so, animated dotted lines trace out the figure and then disappear like angel's dust. As in a Tex Avery cartoon, a pun

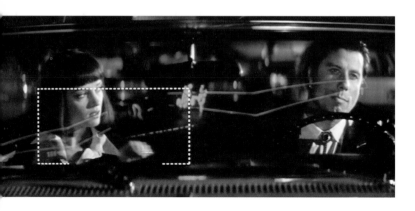

Cartoon technique

is literalised in an image. The film literally writes the fantasy of its creation of imaginary visions onto the movie screen. Indeed, if the animated nature of the square that Mia draws may seem like a reference to filmic imaginary worlds, so does the specific fact that it is a square that is being drawn: a frame within the frame of the movie we're watching, Mia's square reminds us of the ways movies build up fantasy worlds for our delectation.

Similarly, *Pulp Fiction* frequently trades the gritty real-world concern of film noir for realms that approach the dimensions of science-fiction even. Butch's journey with Esmarelda (whose name even sounds fairy-tale like) is only one moment among many of instances of magical transport in which everyday logic is suspended to enable the marvellous to emerge. Take, for instance, the mysterious briefcase which casts an unreal but captivating glow over everyone who peers into it. Even more, take the very way in which a major narrative development concerns the rash of bullets that are discharged at Jules and Vincent from fairly close range and yet fail to hit either of them. Whether or not we take the incident to be a 'miracle' (Jules's interpretation) or a 'freak occurrence' (Vincent's view of the matter), it is apparent that the scene is about a suspension of ordinary laws of reality.

It's not for nothing that the awe-filled look is so central to *Pulp Fiction*, as I noted earlier. What inspires such ocular fascination is something out of the ordinary, something that bewilders or amazes.

Like a rabbit caught in a radish patch, Butch freezes, not knowing what to do

Indeed, for all their differences, we can draw a connection between the cartoon world of *Pulp Fiction* and that of more directly science-fiction directors like George Lucas (the *Star Wars* trilogy) or Steven Spielberg (*E.T.*, *Jurassic Park*, *Close Encounters of the Third Kind*). There is in these directors a concern for building magical kingdoms which characters react to with amazement and into which they adventure (like Indiana Jones, like Vincent at Jack Rabbit Slim's) on a journey that leaves ordinary cares behind. Common to them is a technique for advancing the narrative in which a character looks off-screen with rapture or concern and then we cut to whatever it is they're gazing at.

If *Pulp Fiction* and Disneyland are constructions of imaginary universes that in post-modern style make manifest their artificial nature, we might even directly compare the experience of watching *Pulp Fiction* to visiting a theme park. There is in both activities the sense that the trajectory one follows is made up of a series of individual attractions, each of which sets out to surprise and dazzle. Certainly, many of the moments in *Pulp Fiction* set themselves off from the plot to become stand-alone bits of virtuosity either in the craft of the dialogue, the weirdness of the action – as in the redneck pawnshop – or the show-off quality of the cinematic style. Interestingly, as a fledgling actor, Tarantino used to keep diverse pieces as material for auditions, and as a writer he came up with various narrative bits that would wait around for integration into this or that new story. As he put it himself in a piece he wrote for the *Guardian*, 'I actually approach writing the way an actor approaches acting. I always start with scenes I know I am going to put in and scenes from scripts I never finish. Every script I have written has at least twenty pages that are taken from other things I've done.'[32]

I noted earlier how the narrative structure of *Pulp Fiction* is one that encourages interactivity and involves frequent and abrupt shifts of tone and direction. Like a theme-park ride – but also like the larger theme-park experience in which one goes from ride to ride with interruptions for meals, photos, stage shows, etc. – *Pulp Fiction* moves the spectator from one set piece to the next, creating a roller-coaster experience made up of lulls and high sensations. Earlier, I suggested that the film's obsession with food has to do with a comforting nostalgia for times that are respites from the flux of narrative. Here, it is necessary to add that the snack-break is central to the theme-park experience, where the frenetic consumption of rides is punctuated by leisurely moments of comforting relaxation around culinary replenishment.

And on this narrative ride, the primary goal for the spectator is not to look for meanings (one doesn't interpret Disney so much as live it) but to have an experience, to luxuriate in sensations. Commentators on post-modernity have seen it in a culture of surfaces, 'what you see is what you get'. In some cases, the idea that post-modernity has no depths – and indeed may be opposed to notions of profundity – has led critics to regard its play of experiences as lacking in intensity – what Fredric Jameson in his writings on post-modernity refers to as a 'waning of affect'. But in another way, it might well be that post-modernity also has to do with an intensification of sensory experience – a rendering of a viscerality so intense that it substitutes for all concern with deep meaning. A roller-coaster ride, an explosion in a movie, a virtuoso camera movement are not to be interpreted so much as enjoyed, absorbed as further bits of the society of the spectacle we're immersed in.

Yet, while *Pulp Fiction* is in these respects an intensely *cinematic* film – a film aware of cinematic tradition, a film that plays with cinematic narrative form and becomes at times pure visual display – we need also to entertain ways in which the film isn't just about cinema as an affective

'Vincent is still driving like a striped-ass ape'

outpouring of intense sights and sounds. It may be important, indeed, to emphasise how very literary the film is (it is perhaps significant that its one Academy Award win was for 'Best Original Screenplay'). Although Tarantino is often considered to be someone who lives only inside the world of cinema, television and popular music, it is interesting to note that he himself took literary structure as the model for *Pulp Fiction*:

What I really wanted to do was make a novel on the screen, with characters who enter and exit, who have their own story but who can appear anywhere. I could do what a contemporary writer does: introduce into his book a secondary character who appeared in an earlier book, something like the Glass family that Salinger imagined, and whose members you find move from one novel to the next.[33]

For all its investment in the mass culture visuality of a post-modern experience, *Pulp Fiction* is also a very writerly film, filled with sharp dialogue as much as with action. Conversations such as that between Vincent and Jules over foreign names for US hamburgers become classic bits to be played over by fans (not for nothing is the *Pulp Fiction* soundtrack a blend of musical tracks and great conversation set pieces from the film). As actor Samuel L. Jackson puts it:

Quentin does this unique marriage of theatre and cinema. Film tends to be a show-me thing, and he combines with it the tell-me theatre thing. You never find characters in most films that have so many words, and so many revealing moments where you learn things about them through an oral tradition rather than a visual tradition.[34]

But even in its verbal dimension, *Pulp Fiction* can seem to partake of the post-modern, for so much of its dialogue is, we might say, second-hand, derivative, ersatz. On the one hand, it is a dialogue of allusions (for instance, when hitman Jules decides to give up his career and wander the world in search of meaning as if he were a good old moral modernist, he refers to a TV show as his model: 'You know, like Caine in *Kung Fu*. Just walk from town to town, meet people, get in adventures'). On the other hand, so much of the dialogue in *Pulp Fiction* has to do with people recounting things, speaking of experiences from the past (not only their own past, but cinematic and televisual pasts) as if the thing to be attended to at any moment is not the task at hand but a tale to be told. *Pulp Fiction* is literally literary in that its characters are endlessly telling stories, turning life into narrative. Even the emphasis on dialogue, then, seems to connect to a post-modern concern with reprocessed material and with media of transmission rather than the content of such media and the meaningful messages they might convey.

Broadly speaking, modernist experimentation with narrative – as in, say, Resnais's *Hiroshima, mon amour* and its concern with guilt and memory – intended to make meaningful points: for instance, the European art films of the 60s (Bergman, Antonioni, Fellini, etc.) spoke of the alienation of Man from a confusing universe, the relativity of time in the modern(ist) moment, the absence of a higher metaphysic in a fallen age, the non-communication among human beings, and so on. Modernism quests after meaning even if it imagines that that meaning is not accessible and opts for despairing silence, as in the plays of Samuel Beckett or in philosopher Ludwig Wittgenstein's (in)famous declaration that we must remain silent about things we cannot understand.

In post-modernism, in contrast, the universe is not to be seen as meaningful but is, to put it bluntly, simply *to be seen* – to be experienced in its sheer dazzle, to be lived in the superficiality of its affective sights and sounds. Hence, we witness another important reason for the bits and set pieces in *Pulp Fiction*: beyond their function as allusions to a history of cinema and American popular culture, they float up from the film as so many 'cool' moments, hip instances to be appreciated, ingested, obsessed about, but rarely to be interpreted, rarely to be made meaningful.

To take one example, if in the modernism of *2001* we are to try to figure out what the monolith means – to treat it as a symbol – in *Pulp Fiction*, in contrast, an enigmatic object like the glowing briefcase can never be interpreted: it simply exists and does so as an unexplainable object of fascination. 'What is it? What is it?' the would-be robber Honey Bunny keeps saying as she obsesses over the euphoria on boyfriend Pumpkin's face caught in the briefcase's shine. But we never do learn what it is. To be sure, this does not stop some fans from trying to turn the briefcase into a symbol. Thus, several websites point out that the lock combination on the briefcase is '666', the sign of evil. It must be noted that this doesn't get us very far and doesn't qualify as the sort of deep interpretation modernist art is often subjected to. Perhaps the best interpretation of the contents of the briefcase appears in a Miramax commercial promoting the videotape version of the film, in which it is precisely the tape-for-sale that is revealed as the mesmerising object within! (But we might then note that *Mad* magazine once made fun of modernism by suggesting that the *2001* monolith was the script that would explain the movie!)

'What is it? What is it?'

The enigmas of modernism point toward higher meaning; those of post-modernism stay at the surface and make of the spectator a game-player (one imagines that the Tarantino web designer-cultists are also adept at video games and other puzzles of simulation). Where, for instance, the complications of temporality in a work of modernism like Resnais's *Hiroshima, mon amour* encouraged spectators to reflect on issues of memory and wartime guilt, of personal and national identity, of sexuality and politics, the breaking down of narrative in *Pulp Fiction* becomes a game, a light puzzle to be engaged in playfully, rather than a discourse on, say, perspectives of knowledge, the relativity of human understanding. Not for nothing, again, do some of the *Pulp Fiction* websites devote themselves to figuring out practical issues like the chronology of the film and to poring over details of the film to see if the rules of the game are adhered to. The kind of enigma that drives the *Pulp Fiction* fan on has to do with questions like, 'Do we see Butch drive by the coffee shop on his motorcycle?', when that would violate the temporal logic of the film, rather than what the film means.

Existentialist screenwriter-director Paul Schrader – who concentrates on modernist stories of alienated men trying to make meaning of their fragmented existence – captures some of the distinction between modern and post-modern cinema when in an interview he contrasts his approach to the adaptation of an Elmore Leonard novel with Tarantino's ironic procedures:

After *Pulp Fiction* was a hit, you realized you could do Elmore Leonard the way Elmore Leonard is meant to be done. … There is a big difference [between me and Tarantino]. I mean, I'm really of the existential tradition, the 20th-century tradition. Tarantino is tying into the ironic hero. I know the existential hero's in trouble and I know this century is almost over. But I don't know how nourishing the ironic hero can be. … The existential dilemma is, 'Should I live?' And the ironic answer is, 'Does it matter?' Everything in the ironic world has quotation marks around it. You don't actually kill somebody; you 'kill' them. It doesn't really matter if you put the baby in front of the runaway car because it's only a 'baby' and it's only a 'car.'[35]

This is not to say that one couldn't come up with a way to interpret *Pulp Fiction*. In fact, there is a tradition of writing that would extract from the film a thematics of redemption. Janet Maslin's discussion of the film in the context of the offerings of the New York Film Festival gives perhaps the clearest rendition of this thematic reading:

The unusual chronology of Quentin Tarantino's film accentuates the way his characters' decisions can change their destinies, even as their futures are seen falling into place. Circular in structure, the movie closes with the image of a man [Vincent] who is fated to die ... because he has not understood how to save his own life. (Following another character along a newly adopted path of righteousness would have made all the difference in the world.) A vision like this elevates *Pulp Fiction* well above its own ebullient sense of fun, even establishing it as the anti-*Gump* [a reference to *Forrest Gump*, the film that received the major Oscars in the race with *Pulp Fiction*].[36]

In a review like this, interpretation works to extract a Message whose communication to audiences it assumes is the film's singular purpose. The translation of the whole texture and textuality of an artwork into a verbal message means that tone, feel, the sensuousness of form, and so on, all have to be left behind. In the case of *Pulp Fiction*, it is easy to feel that such transformation of the filmic work into a parable – for example, you must redeem yourself and change your ways! – misses so much of what is going on in the experience of the film. First of all, there is little need for an act of interpretive excavation, since the theme of Jules's redemption is an explicit plot turn in the film; you don't need to work at it to get it. Since Jules himself interprets the bullets missing him, the message is there in full evidence, already expressed for us. It then becomes necessary to decide if in fact the transmission of this theme is indeed the point of the film, its reason for being.

    In particular, we might want to note how much of the Jules-redemption plot is rendered as a curiosity, one more part of the weird turn of events in a film given over to detours and unpredictability.

Additionally, Jules's conversion is rendered comic, if not downright ironic, by its treatment: for example, as I noted earlier, this moment of seeming high seriousness is still presented in terms of pop-culture allusions (Jules comparing himself to Caine in the TV show *Kung Fu*) and in terms of the Cool that Jules has always had. In her essay on the film, bell hooks even suggests that the seriousness of Jules's message is undone by his somewhat campy depiction throughout the film:

No doubt that retro hairdo he sports throughout the film keeps him from charting a new journey. It's his own signifying monkey. No matter how serious Jules's rap, that hair always intervenes to let the audience know to not take him too seriously. That hair is kinda like another character in the film. Talking back to Jules as he talks to us, it undermines his words every step of the way.[37]

It is not surprising, as I also noted earlier, that until the very last minute, we are not sure if Jules will kill Pumpkin and Honey Bunny in the diner: for all the avowed announcement of a conversion on his part, Jules is still caught up until the last moment in the film's flirtation with the unexpected, with its undoing of all fixed moral perspectives.

Certainly, one can decide to interpret *Pulp Fiction*, but only by not seeing it as experience, as game, as visuality, as cinema. To be sure, to

Jules's retro hairdo

view *Pulp Fiction* cinematically in this way can create its own moral problems: do we necessarily want to retreat into the obsessions of spectacle when there is so much to be done in the world (including living it)? This is the question some critics of the film have raised, condemning what is taken to be the film's supposedly irresponsible lack of meaning, its empty play with form, its art for art's sake. Between the options of finding a message in the film and of luxuriating in an experiential lack of messages, there is for these critics the possibility of taking *Pulp Fiction*'s lack of a moral to be itself a message about the film's immorality as they see it. Such, for instance, is the substance of an intensely virulent attack on the film in the *Los Angeles Times* by conservative art critic Roger Shattuck, 'The Alibi of Art: What Baudelaire, Nabokov, and Quentin Tarantino Have in Common'. For Shattuck, it is the film's absence of message that is its problem:

Pulp Fiction does not satirize our media culture. It succumbs willingly to that culture, celebrates it, exploits it, and successfully spreads its meaningless violence and jokeyness across all human lives shown. ... The cinematic attitude that everything is a spectacle, a camera shot or a dream sequence now applies to all life, even our own. No clue in the movie sends any different message ... [*Pulp Fiction*] does set out to eliminate the reference point of reality. In that affectless world, coolness reveals itself as a form of autism.[38]

Ironically, for a moralist like Shattuck, it is the film's unreality which makes it have an all-too-real effect in the real world, its lack of meaning becoming its meaning:

Everyone comes through desensitized to violence and a little more detached from one's own encounters with real life. *Pulp Fiction* has a message: What a lark crime can be! ... I believe that this allegedly new form of experience, when isolated from the demands of 'real life' can lead us to a new idolatry – the idolatry of art. We are tempted, not religiously but commercially, to accept the alluring category of the aesthetic whose cool detachment is made to look as if it will wash away everyone's sins and excesses. The consequences of that illusion will be very destructive … [Responsible art] deserves to be protected with all our powers from those who would borrow its mantle to protect and ennoble displays of unredeemed depravity and violence.[39]

Whatever one thinks of a position like Shattuck's – hysterically extreme? a necessary balm in our callous age? – what his virulent attack makes clear is how the critique as well as appreciation of post-modern superficiality derives from decisions one has made (whether consciously or not) about the ways cultural works relate to real-life behaviour. What one decides will determine what one thinks of a film like *Pulp Fiction* and means that people with differing views will not easily be able to share their perspectives. Like the allusions in the film, *Pulp Fiction* itself is either a film you get or you don't. Some people luxuriate in its meaninglessness, some people find its meaninglessness to be the symptom if not the origin of major social ills, others find a meaningfulness in a message of redemption. It is this lack of agreement that is perhaps itself a mark of *Pulp Fiction*'s place as a post-modern work.

'And now the end is near' (Frank Sinatra, and Elvis Presley Reprise)

In the last scene of the script for *Pulp Fiction*, there's an interesting example of the bewildered questioning at plot twists that I've suggested is enacted by characters in the film and shared perhaps by many audience members. At the diner, Vincent emerges once again from a bathroom to find Honey Bunny and Jules in a 'Mexican stand-off'. Jules has just explained to Honey Bunny and Pumpkin that he is saving them because he is 'in a transitional period' (itself an ironically undercutting way to describe conversion), and the script immediately has Vincent burst in with 'What the fuck's goin' on here?' and then 'What the hell's going on, Jules?'

Even if Vincent's declarations of bewilderment didn't make it into the film itself, they float in the air of the scene – indeed, of the whole film.

Like Honey Bunny's repeated wonder about the briefcase – 'What is it? What is it?', 'Goddamit, what is it?' – questions flow through *Pulp Fiction* and the film takes pleasure in the undecidability of its answers. Jules – and some critics along with him – may have located a final meaning in a message of redemption. But Jules's discovery of a theme is not the final moment of the film. With the stand-off over, Vincent suggests that he and Jules better leave the diner, and Jules assents. At the door, with an almost choreographed unison, they both look around and ostentatiously stick their big guns in the waistbands of their bermuda shorts, Jules participating as much as Vincent. As the script puts it in its last line:

> Then, to the amazement of the Patrons, the Waitresses, the Cooks, the Busboys, and the Manager, these two bad-ass dudes – wearing UC Santa Cruz and 'I'm with Stupid' T-shirts, swim trunks, thongs and packing .45 Automatics – walk out of the coffee shop together without saying a word.

Amazed bystanders. Two hip guys who can maintain cool (even with inappropriate dress). Style winning out over substance. This is how the film ends. More than any explicit message, this is the point of *Pulp Fiction*. This is why it is a phenomenon.

'Bad-ass dudes'

Notes

1 David Gritten, 'Tarantino the Icon Captures Britain', *Los Angeles Times*, 4 February 1995, p. F1.

2 Tarantino quoted in Gerald Perry (ed.), *Quentin Tarantino: Interviews* (Jackson, MS: University Press of Mississippi, 1998), p. 32.

3 Robin Wood, *Sexual Politics and Narrative Film: Hollywood and Beyond* (New York: Columbia University Press, 1998), p. 338.

4 Fintan O'Toole, 'Bloody Minded; Tarantino: The High Priest of Sadistic Moral Vacuity', *Guardian*, 3 February 1995, p. T16.

5 Jack Mathews, 'Can 200 Critics Be Wrong? (Maybe)', *Los Angeles Times*, 26 December 1994, p. F1.

6 Dave Wadsworth, 'Tarantino Too Hip for His Own Good', *Denver Post*, 6 November 1994, magazine section, p. 19.

7 Jean-Pierre Deloux, *Quentin Tarantino … fils de pulp* (Paris: Editions Fleuve Noir, 1998), pp. 244–5.

8 Pat Dowell and John Fried, 'Pulp Friction: Two Shots at Quentin Tarantino's *Pulp Fiction*', *Cineaste*, vol. 21 no. 3, 1995, p. 5.

9 Sarah Kerr, 'Rain Man: *Pulp Fiction*', *New York Review of Books*, 6 April 1995, p. 23.

10 Roger Ebert, 'One-Stop Mayhem Shop: *Pulp Fiction* Hurtles into Bizarre Universe', *Chicago Sun-Times*, 14 October 1994, Weekend Plus section, p. 43.

11 Tarantino quoted in Andrew Pulver, 'The Movie Junkie; the Critics Hated it, the Audience Hurled Abuse: Stand by for Quentin Tarantino's *Pulp Fiction*', *Guardian*, 19 September 1994, Features, p. 78.

12 Sharon Willis, 'The Fathers Watch the Boys' Room: Race and Masculinity in the Work of Quentin Tarantino', *Camera Obscura*, no. 32, May 1995, pp. 41–73; and '"Style", Posture, and Idiom: Quentin Tarantino's Figures of Masculinity', in Linda Williams and Christine Gledhill (eds), *Film Studies* (London: Edward Arnold, forthcoming).

13 Jeff Dawson, *Quentin Tarantino: The Cinema of Cool* (London and New York: Applause Books, 1995), p. 128.

14 Ibid., p. 156.

15 Manohla Dargis, 'Pulp Instincts', *Sight & Sound*, vol. 4 no. 5, May 1994, p. 8.

16 Joe Engel, 'Tim Roth Jumps from van Gogh to *Dogs*', *New York Times*, 22 November 1992, Arts and Leisure, section 2, p. 18.

17 In a review of *Jackie Brown*, columnist Steven Hunter offers a typology of kinds of cool that show up in that Tarantino film (and in the attitude of the director himself), and many of these are present in *Pulp Fiction*, too: 'urban street cool', 'beautiful-women-who-are-also-wise-cool', 'ruthless-cop-cool', 'old-coot-cool', 'wasted-junkie-white-trash-cool', 'surfer-bimbo-cool', 'vid-geek-turned-director-cool'. See Steven Hunter, '*Jackie Brown*: Cool at a Fever Pitch', *Washington Post*, 25 December 1997, p. C1.

18 Dowell and Fried, 'Pulp Friction', p. 4.

19 Alan Barnes and Marcus Hearn, *Tarantino, A to Zed: The Films of Quentin Tarantino* (London: Batsford, 1996), p. 34.

20 Willis '"Style", Posture, and Idiom'.

21 Tarantino quoted in Perry (ed.), *Interviews*, p. 101.

22 Andrew Anthony, 'Tarantino's Main Man: You Can Call Him "Nigga" … Just Don't Call Him "Nigger"', *Observer*, 8 March 1998, p. 6.

23 Devon Jackson, 'Quentin Tarantino's Negro Problem and Hollywood's', *Village Voice*, vol. 40 no. 13, 28 March 1995, p. 39.

24 bell hooks, '*Pulp Fiction*', in *Reel to Real: Race, Sex, and Class at the Movies* (London and New York: Routledge, 1996), pp. 48–9.

25 Jackson, 'Quentin Tarantino's Negro Problem', p. 40.

26 Anonymous, 'Guns 'n Poses: Profile – Quentin Tarantino', *Sunday Telegraph*, 8 March 1998, Comment section, p. 35.

27 Deloux, *Quentin Tarantino … fils de pulp*, pp.13–14.

28 Michael Denning, *The Cultural Front: The Laboring of American Culture in the Twentieth Century* (London and New York: Verso, 1996).

29 Deloux, *Quentin Tarantino … fils de pulp*, p.14.

30 Claudia Eller, 'Tristar Passes on *Fiction* but No One's Mad', *Los Angeles Times*, 27 June 1993, Sunday Calendar section, p. 25.

31 Amanda Lipman, 'Pulp Fiction', *Sight & Sound*, vol. 4 no. 11, November 1994, p. 51.

32 Quentin Tarantino, 'Movie Masterclass: Quentin Tarantino on *Pulp Fiction*', *Guardian*, 26 May 1994, p. T8.

33 Tarantino in Perry (ed.), *Interviews*, p. 81.

34 Bob Thompson, interview with Samuel L. Jackson, *Toronto Sun*, 16 October 1994, Sunday Showcase, p. S3.

35 Roger Ebert, 'Screenwriters Schrader, Tarantino Hot with Different Heroes', *Denver Post*, 23 February 1997, Section A, p. G-01.

36 Janet Maslin, 'When Fate Is Calling the Tune', *New York Times*, 16 October 1994, Section 2, p. 13.

37 bell hooks, '*Pulp Fiction*', p. 50.

38 Roger Shattuck, 'The Alibi of Art: What Baudelaire, Nabokov, and Quentin Tarantino Have in Common', *Los Angeles Times Book Review*, 26 April 1998, p. 3.

39 Ibid.

Credits

Pulp Fiction

USA
1994

Director
Quentin Tarantino
Producer
Lawrence Bender
Screenplay
Quentin Tarantino
Stories by
Quentin Tarantino,
Roger Avary
Director of Photography
Andrzej Sekula
Editor
Sally Menke
Production Designer
David Wasco

©Miramax Films
Production Companies
Miramax Films present
A Band Apart and Jersey
Films production
a film by Quentin Tarantino
Executive Producers
Danny DeVito, Michael
Shamberg, Stacey Sher
Co-executive Producers
Bob Weinstein, Harvey
Weinstein, Richard N.
Gladstein
Production Accountant
Julia Zane
Production Auditor
Angelique A. Costanza
Assistant Accountant
Zane

Accounting Assistant
Abigail Sheiner
Accounting Intern
Cynthia Harding
Production Co-ordinator
Anna-Lisa Nilsson
**Assistant Production
Co-ordinator**
Cheryl Cain
Co-ordinator for Miramax
Cathy Agcayab Ragona
Production Manager
Paul Hellerman
Location Manager
Robert Earl Craft
**Assistant Location
Manager**
John A. Johnston
Location Assistant
Haley B. Sweet
**Post-production
Supervisor**
Heidi Vogel
**Post-production
Co-ordinator**
Kara Mazzola
**Post-production
Accountant**
Angelique A. Costanza
**Assistant to the Producer
– Post-production**
Courtney McDonnell
**Post-production
Assistant**
Ben Parker
Post-production Intern
Liam Curtin
Production Secretary
Bradley Morris

**Key Office Production
Assistant**
James 'Chip' Weis
Assistant to the Producer
Toni Baffo
**Set Production
Assistants**
Iain Jones, Sarah Kelly,
Thomas Magno, Stevie
Maislen, Tanya Richardson
**Office Production
Assistants**
Jay Beattie, Nathan
Easterling, Alicia Magnant,
Francesca McCattery,
Tristan Sharp
**Production Legal
Services**
Carlos Goodman, Lichter,
Grossman & Nichols, Inc
Music Legal Services
Codikow & Carroll
Miramax Legal
Vicki Cherkas
**Immigration Legal
Services**
Robert Fraade, Esq.
Labour Legal Services
Richard W. Kopenhefer,
Loeb and Loeb
Completion Guarantors
Film Finances, Inc,
Kurt Woolner
Clearance Supervisor
Donald Asher
1st Assistant Director
Francis R. 'Sam' Mahony III
2nd Assistant Director
Kelly Kiernan

2nd 2nd Assistant Director
John 'Crash' Hyde Jr

Additional 2nd 2nd Assistant Director
William Paul Clark

Assistant to the Director
Victoria Lucai

Script Supervisor
Martin Kitrosser

Casting
Ronnie Yeskel,
Gary M. Zuckerbrod

ADR Voice Casting
Barbara Harris

Casting Associate
Ruth Lambert

Extras Casting
Rainbow Casting

Second Unit Photography
Alan Sherrod

Camera Operator
Michael Levine

1st Assistant Cameraman
Ziad Doueiri

2nd Assistant Cameraman
Gregory C. Smith

Camera Loader
Angelo De La Cruz

Key Grip
Mark Shane Davis

Best Boy Grip
Robert W. Meckler

Key Rigging Grip
Michael Stocks

Dolly Grip
Alan Parr

Grips
Randy Verdugo, James P.
Jones II, C. Roy Nigra,
Christopher Ahern,
Robert Studenny

Steadicam Operator
Robert Gorelick

Additional Steadicam Operator
John Nuler

Steadicam 1st Assistant
Joe Ritter

Gaffer
Vance Trussell

Best Boy Electric
Anthony Hall

Key Rigging Gaffer
Marc Meisenheimer

Electricians
Christopher Loring, Robert
Lewbel, Bruce Jagoda,
Michael Palmer

Video Playback Operator
Larry Markart

Unit Still Photographer
Linda R. Chen

Special Effects Co-ordinator
Larry Fioritto

Special Effects
Wesley Mattox, Stephen
DeLollis, Pat Domenico

Chief Graphic Designer
Gerald Martinez

Graphic Designer
Chris Cullen

Character Artist
Russell Vossler

Assembly Editor
Jere P. Huggins

1st Assistant Editor
Tatiana S. Riegel

Second Assistant Editors
Katie Mack, Ray Neapolitan

Assistant Editor
Donald Likovich

Apprentice Editors
Andrew Dickler, John
Sosnovski

Art Director
Charles Collum

Art Department Co-ordinator
Emily Wolfe

Assistant Art Directors
Samantha Gore

Set Designers
Daniel Bradford, Jacek
Lisiewicz

Set Decorator
Sandy Reynolds-Wasco

Lead Man
Peter Borck

Assistant Decorator
Liz Chiz

On-set Dresser
McPherson O. Downs

Set Dressers
Joseph Grafmuller, Daniel
Rothenberg

Charge Scenic Artist
Chris L. Winslow

Swing Gang
Steven Ingrassia, Ed Martin
II, Maryann Matanic,
Sally Reed

Property Master
Jonathan Hodges

Assistant Property Master
John Felgate

Prop Food Stylist
Showgrits, Jean Hodges
Buyer
Ellen Brill
Construction Co-ordinator
Brian Markey
Construction Foreman
Ray Maxwell
Construction Location Foreman
Shane Hawkins
Construction Estimator
Chris Scher
Carpenters
Gary L. Brennan, Joseph Donti, Tim Glueckert, B. Harris, Jose Jimenez, Adam Markey, Michael McGettigan, Dave Mendelson, Mark Peters, Wayne Springfield
Lead Painter
Marc Gillson
Painters
Giuseppe Maini III, Amy Skiumsby, Greg Wilson
Costume Designer
Betsy Heimann
Assistant Costume Designer
Mary Claire Hannan
Costume Supervisor
Jacqueline Aronson
Costumers
Kristin Dangl, Marilyn Pachasa, Patia Prouty
Key Make-up Artist
Michelle Bühler

Special Make-up Effects
Kurtzman, Nicotero and Berger EFX Group, Inc.
Make-up Effects Crew
Wayne Toth, David Smith, Ted Haines, Douglas Noe, Tom Bellissimo, Erin Haggerty
Key Hair Supervisor
Audree Futterman
Assistant Make-up/Hair
Cristina Bartolucci
Hair Designer
Iain Jones
Assistant Hair
Linda Arnold
Wigmaker
Bill Fletcher
Hair Extensions Design
Piny of Beverly Hills
Titles/Opticals
Pacific Title
Colour Timer
Michael Stanwick
Music Supervisors
Karyn Rachtman
MCA Records:
Kathy Nelson
Assistants to Music Supervisor
Billy Gottlieb, Kristen Becht
Music Co-ordinator for Mind Your Music
Mary Ramos
Music Consultants
Chuck Kelley, Laura Lovelace
Music Editor
Rolf Johnson

Soundtrack
"Misirlou" by Fred Wise, Milton Leeds, S.K. Russell, Nicholas Roubanis, performed by Dick Dale & His Del-Tones; "Strawberry Letter #23" by Shuggie Otis, performed by The Brothers Johnson; "Bustin' Surfboards" by Gerald Sanders, Jesse Sanders, Norman Sanders, Leonard Delaney, performed by The Tornadoes; "Son of a Preacher Man" by John Hurley, Ronnie Wilkins, performed by Dusty Springfield; "Lonesome Town" by Baker Knight, performed by Ricky Nelson; "Rumble" by F.L. Wray Sr, M. Cooper, performed by Link Wray and His Ray Men; "Teenagers in Love" by William Rosenauer, performed by Woody Thorne; "Girl, You'll Be a Woman Soon" by Neil Diamond, performed by Urge Overkill; "Flowers on the Wall" by Lewis DeWitt, performed by The Statler Brothers; "Comanche" by/performed by The Revels; "Jungle Boogie" by Ronald Bell, Claydes Smith, George Brown, Robert Mickens, Donald Boyce, Richard Westfield, Dennis Thomas, Robert Bell, performed by Kool & The Gang; "Let's

Stay Together" by Al Green, Al Jackson Jr, Willie Mitchell, performed by Al Green; "Bullwinkle Part II" by Dennis Rose, Ernest Furrow, performed by The Centurians; "Waitin' in School" by Johnny Burnette, Dorsey Burnette, performed by Gary Shorelle, produced by Joseph Vitarelli, Nick Viterelli; "Ace of Spades" by F.L. Wray Sr, M. Cooper, performed by Link Wray; "Since I First Met You" by H.B. Barnum, performed by The Robins; "You Never Can Tell" by/performed by Chuck Berry; "If Love Is a Red Dress (Hang Me in Rags)" by/performed by Maria McKee; "Out of Limits" by Michael Gordon, performed by The Marketts; "Surf Rider" by Bob Bogle, Nole Edwards, Don Wilson, performed by The Lively Ones; "Coffee Shop Music"

Production Sound Mixer
Ken King
Boom Operator
Larry Scharf
Re-recording Mixers
Rick Ash, Dean A. Zupancic
Pre-dub Mixer
Ezra Dweck
Dubbing Recordist
Larry Pitman
PDL
Ivan Johnson

Supervising Sound Editor
Stephen H. Flick
Sound Editors
David Bartlett, Dean Beville, G.W. Brown, Avram Dean Gold, John Hulsman, Patricio Libenson, Richard Marx, Stewart Nelsen, Charles E. Smith, Scott Weber
Assistant Sound Editors
Jeena M. Phelps, Dana Gustafson
Negative Cutter
I.C.E. Negative Cutting
ADR Mixer
Jeff Courtie
Supervising ADR Editor
Judee Flick
Foley
Joan Rowe, Catherine Rowe
Foley Mixer
Ezra Dweck
Transportation Co-ordinator
Derek Raser
Transportation Captain
J.T. Thayer II
Driver/Mechanic
Steve Earle
Production Van Driver
David Joseph
Drivers
Scotty Goudreau, Don Feeney, Tracy 'Ace' Thielen, Gregg Willis, Paul Burlin, John Key, Alonzo Brown Jr, Bruce Callahan, Earl 'Mr Blonde' Thielen, Glenn McCraven

Water Truck Driver
George Sack
Driver Production Assistants
Derek N. Alff 'DNA', Suzy Mae Martin, Richard C. Middleton
Set Security
C.A.S.T. Security, Ruben Cortez (Supervisor)
Production Catering
Mario's Catering
Craft Service
Derek Hurd
Assistant Craft Service
Michael Haddod
Stunt Co-ordinator
Ken Lesco
Stunt Players
Cameron, Chris Doyle, Marcia Holley, Terry Jackson, Melvin Jones, Linda Kaye, Hubie Kerns Jr, Scott McElroy, Dennis 'Danger' Madalone
Stunt Safety
Matthew Avila
Stand-ins
Cameron, Cullen Chambers, Scott Johnston, Rory K. Dauson, Jeffrey Stephan, Gloria Hylton
Unit Publicist
Deborah Wuliger
Film Extract
The Losers (1970)

Cast
John Travolta
Vincent Vega
Samuel L. Jackson
Jules Winnfield
Uma Thurman
Mia Wallace
Harvey Keitel
Winston, 'The Wolf'
Tim Roth
'Pumpkin'
Amanda Plummer
Yolanda, 'Honey Bunny'
Maria de Medeiros
Fabienne
Ving Rhames
Marsellus Wallace
Eric Stoltz
Lance
Rosanna Arquette
Jody
Christopher Walken
Captain Koons
Bruce Willis
Butch Coolidge
Paul Calderon
Paul
Bronagh Gallagher
Trudi
Peter Greene
Zed
Stephen Hibbert
The Gimp
Angela Jones
Esmarelda Villa Lobos

Phil LaMarr
Marvin
Robert Ruth
coffee shop
Julia Sweeney
Raquel
Quentin Tarantino
Jimmie
Frank Whaley
Brett
Duane Whitaker
Maynard
Laura Lovelace
waitress
Burr Steers
Roger
Jerome Patrick Hoban
Ed Sullivan
Michael Gilden
Phillip Morris page
Gary Shorelle
Ricky Nelson
Susan Griffiths
Marilyn Monroe
Eric Clark
James Dean
Josef Pilato
Dean Martin
Brad Parker
Jerry Lewis
Steve Buscemi
Buddy Holly
Lorelei Leslie
Mamie Van Doren
Emil Sitka
'hold hands you love birds'
Brenda Hillhouse
Butch's mother
Chandler Lindauer
young Butch

Sy Sher
Klondike
Robert Ruth
sportscaster 1
Rich Turner
sportscaster 2
Don Blakely
Wilson's trainer
Carl Allen
dead Floyd Wilson
Karen Maruyama
gawker 1
Kathy Griffin
herself, gawker 2
Venessia Valentino
pedestrian
Linda Kaye
shot lady
Alexis Arquette
fourth man
Venessia Valentino
Bonnie
Lawrence Bender
long hair yuppie-scum

13,893 feet
154 minutes

Dolby Stereo Digital SR
Colour by
DeLuxe
Anamorphic [Panavision]

Credits compiled by Markku
Salmi, BFI Filmographic Unit

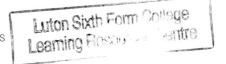

Bibliography

BOOKS

Barnes, Alan and Marcus Hearn, *Tarantino, A to Zed: The Films of Quentin Tarantino* (London: Batsford, 1996).

Bernard, Jami, *Quentin Tarantino: The Man and His Movies* (New York: HarperCollins, 1995).

Clarkson, Wensley, *Quentin Tarantino: Shooting from the Hip* (Woodstock, NY:The Overlook Press, 1995).

Dawson, Jeff, *Quentin Tarantino: The Cinema of Cool* (London and New York: Applause Books, 1995).

Deloux, Jean-Pierre, *Quentin Tarantino … fils de pulp* (Paris: Editions Fleuve Noir, 1998).

Perry, Gerald (ed.), *Quentin Tarantino: Interviews* (Jackson, MS: University Press of Mississippi, 1998).

Surcouf, Yannick, *Quentin Tarantino: d'Alabama à Killing Zoe* (Paris: Editions Méréal, 1998).

Tarantino, Quentin, *Pulp Fiction: A Quentin Tarantino Screenplay* (London: Faber & Faber, 1996).

Woods, Paul A., *King Pulp: The Wild World of Quentin Tarantino* (New York: Thunder's Mouth Press, 1996).

ESSAYS AND SHORT CRITICISM

Artforum, vol. 33 no. 7, March 1995. 'Pulp the Hype on the QT', pp. 66–7, 108, 110. Forum on Tarantino with Gary Indiana, bell hooks, Jeanne Silverthorne, Dennis Cooper, Robin Wood.

Brooker, Peter and Will, 'Pulpmodernism: Tarantino's Affirmative Action', in Deborah Cartmell, I. Q. Hunter, Heidi Kaye and Imelda Whelehan (eds), *Pulping Fictions: Consuming Culture across the Literature/Media Divide* (London and Chicago: Pluto Press, 1996), pp. 135–51.

Burchill, Julie, 'Shooting from the Hip' [review of *Pulp Fiction*],*Sunday Times* (London), 23 October 1994, Features section.

Crouch, Stanley, 'Pulp Friction: Director Quentin Tarantino's Movies Are Best Known for Their Wit and Mayhem, but What You Don't Hear about Them Is Their Original Take on Race', *Los Angeles Times*, 16 October 1994, Calendar section, p. 5.

Dargis, Manohla, 'Pulp Instincts', *Sight & Sound*, vol. 4 no. 5, May 1994, pp. 6–9.

Davis, Todd and Kenneth Womack, 'Shepherding the Weak: The Ethics of Redemption in Quentin Tarantino's *Pulp Fiction*', *Literature/Film Quarterly*, vol. 26 no. 1, 1998, pp. 60–7.

Dinshaw, Carolyn, 'Getting Medieval, *Pulp Fiction*, Foucault, and the Use of the Past', in Dinshaw, *Getting Medieval: Sexualities and Communities, Pre- and Post Modern* (Durham: Duke University Press, 1999), pp. 183–206.

Dowell, Pat and John Fried, 'Pulp Friction: Two Shots at Quentin Tarantino's *Pulp Fiction*', *Cineaste*, vol. 21 no. 3, 1995, pp. 4–7.

hooks, bell, '*Pulp Fiction*', in *Reel to Real: Race, Sex, and Class at the Movies* (London and New York: Routledge, 1996), pp. 47–51.

Jackson, Devon, 'Quentin Tarantino's Negro Problem and Hollywood's', *Village Voice*, vol. 40 no. 13, 28 March 1996, pp. 39–40.

Kimball, A. Samuel, '"Bad-Ass Dudes" in *Pulp Fiction*: Homophobia and the Counterphobic Idealization of Women', *Quarterly Review of Film and Video*, vol. 16 no. 2, 1997, pp. 171–92.

Macaulay, Scott, 'Producing *Pulp*', *Filmmaker*, vol. 2 no. 4, Summer 1994, pp. 16, 61.

Palmer, R. Barton, 'Quentin Tarantino', *International Dictionary of Films and Filmmakers, Vol. 2: Directors*, third edition (Detroit: St James Press, 1977), pp. 980–2.

Seddon, Fred, 'Some Truths about *Pulp Fiction*', *Film and Philosophy*, vol. 4 1997, pp. 20–6.

Tarantino, Quentin, 'On *Pulp Fiction*', *Sight & Sound*, vol. 4 no. 11, November 1994, pp. 16–19.

Willis, Sharon, 'The Fathers Watch the Boys' Room: Race and Masculinity in the Work of Quentin Tarantino', *Camera Obscura*, no. 32, May 1995, pp. 41–73.

Willis, Sharon, '"Style", Posture, and Idiom: Quentin Tarantino's Figures of Masculinity', in Linda Williams and Christine Gledhill (eds), *Film Studies* (London: Edward Arnold, forthcoming).

Also Published

L'Argent
Kent Jones (1999)

Blade Runner
Scott Bukatman (1997)

Blue Velvet
Michael Atkinson (1997)

Caravaggio
Leo Bersani & Ulysse Dutoit (1999)

Crash
Iain Sinclair (1999)

The Crying Game
Jane Giles (1997)

Dead Man
Jonathan Rosenbaum (2000)

Don't Look Now
Mark Sanderson (1996)

Easy Rider
Lee Hill (1996)

The Exorcist
Mark Kermode (1997, 2nd edn 1998)

Independence Day
Michael Rogin (1998)

Last Tango in Paris
David Thompson (1998)

Once Upon a Time in America
Adrian Martin (1998)

The Right Stuff
Tom Charity (1997)

Salò or The 120 Days of Sodom
Gary Indiana (2000)

Seven
Richard Dyer (1999)

The Terminator
Sean French (1996)

Thelma & Louise
Marita Sturken (2000)

The Thing
Anne Billson (1997)

The 'Three Colours' Trilogy
Geoff Andrew (1998)

Titanic
David M. Lubin (1999)

The Wings of the Dove
Robin Wood (1999)

Women on the Verge of a Nervous Breakdown
Peter William Evans (1996)

WR – Mysteries of the Organism
Raymond Durgnat (1999)

WITHDRAWN

Forthcoming

Do the Right Thing
Ed Guerrero (2001)

Star Wars
Peter Wollen (2001)